Cat Counsellor

www.**booksattransworld**.co.uk

Also by Vicky Halls

Cat Confidential
Cat Detective

CAT COUNSELLOR

VICKY HALLS

BANTAM PRESS

LONDON · TORONTO · SYDNEY · AUCKLAND · JOHANNESBURG

TRANSWORLD PUBLISHERS
61–63 Uxbridge Road, London W5 5SA
a division of The Random House Group Ltd

RANDOM HOUSE AUSTRALIA (PTY) LTD
20 Alfred Street, Milsons Point, Sydney,
New South Wales 2061, Australia

RANDOM HOUSE NEW ZEALAND LTD
18 Poland Road, Glenfield, Auckland 10, New Zealand

RANDOM HOUSE SOUTH AFRICA (PTY) LTD
Isle of Houghton, Corner of Boundary Road & Carse O'Gowrie, Houghton 2198, South Africa

RANDOM HOUSE PUBLISHERS INDIA PRIVATE LIMITED
301 World Trade Tower, Hotel Intercontinental Grand Complex,
Barakhamba Lane, New Delhi 110 001, India

Published 2006 by Bantam Press
a division of Transworld Publishers

A catalogue record for this book is available from the British Library.
ISBN 9780593055649 (from Jan 07)
ISBN 0593055640

Typeset in 12/15.75pt Cochin by
Falcon Oast Graphic Art Ltd

Printed and bound in Great Britain by
Mackays of Chatham plc, Chatham, Kent

1 3 5 7 9 10 8 6 4 2

Papers used by Transworld Publishers are natural, recyclable products made from wood grown
in sustainable forests. The manufacturing processes conform to the environmental
regulations of the country of origin.

This book is dedicated to the memory of
Joan and Eric Pattle, my mum and dad.

CONTENTS

ACKNOWLEDGEMENTS

I would like to thank Mary Pachnos, my wonderful agent, and Francesca Liversidge, my editor at Transworld, for their continued support, advice and good humour. Tamzin Barber, a brilliant Cat Counsellor in the making, helped me so much with research, as did Sharon Cole, Robin Walker, Vicki Adams, Rozanna Malcolm and Clive Butler. My clients, as always, have been consistently wonderful and every one has contributed in some way to this book. I would also like to thank Peter who continues to look after Lucy, Annie and Bink in Cornwall. I couldn't do the work I do without his input and support. Last but not least are Mangus and Charles, the other two sides of my own eternal triangle. Thank you, Mangus, for sitting by my computer constantly and keeping me sane. Thank you, Charles, for just being you.

Introduction

FOR SOME YEARS NOW, AS A CAT BEHAVIOUR COUNSELLOR, I have trekked around the country visiting owners and their cats. All the cats have one thing in common. They are behaving in such a way as to cause a great deal of angst and distress to their owners. They may be attacking next-door's Persian, biting the postman or pooing on the duvet. The problem in question can be just about anything, even 'my cat loves me too much' or 'my cat doesn't love me enough'. My job is to unravel the mystery, identify the underlying issue and, God willing and with a *lot* of co-operation from the client, put it right. It is such a bizarre way to earn a living (cat psychiatry was never discussed by my school's career adviser) that it is almost inevitable that a certain amount of objective analysis must take place. After all, I do spend a great deal of time driving around the country with nothing better to do than muse on the vagaries of my profession. Are cats getting more stressed? Are there more problems now than in the past or are we just more amenable to discussing them? Have we crammed too many cats onto this tiny island of ours? Are they getting stressed by each other? Are we expecting too much of them? Is this our fault? Is seven hours really a reasonable amount of time to get from Kent to North London? (Sorry. The driving in this job can be unbearable.)

I recently produced some statistics to illustrate particular points being made in a seminar for pet behaviour counsellors. My quest was merely to break down the workload of three consecutive years to see what percentage of cases each common problem represented. As I crunched the numbers I started to disappear down a completely different avenue quite by accident. I was vaguely searching through my copious notes for answers to the question 'Are there any common causes here?' and I found something quite astonishing. Fifty per cent of the problem behaviour was exhibited as a direct result of something specific to the owner/cat relationship. The remaining 50 per cent was exacerbated by the same thing. Now this in itself may not seem like such a revelation but, believe me, it is. Think about it. If you have read *Cat Confidential* and *Cat Detective*, my two previous books, you will know by now that cat behaviour counselling is all about changing the environment and changing the way the owner interacts with the cat. I don't train the cats or enforce my will upon them. I work around them and, as if by magic, they reform. I have avoided for many years apportioning blame for the cats' misdemeanours; this is never productive and certainly not a positive way to get the owner on your side. Maybe that's why I've never actually looked at the facts this way round before. I've always known that owners can greatly influence the behaviour of their cats but I don't think I ever sat down and really thought about what a significant and widespread issue it really is. Not that I want to imply in any way that owners with messed-up cats are bad owners. Quite the contrary; they are usually good, loving, caring and intelligent people trying desperately to do the right thing. Cats unfortunately can lead us up the garden path sometimes with their enigmatic ways, and loving them as much as we do can be a problem.

I have a confession. Recently I succumbed to enormous pressure and agreed to adopt a cat to live with me in my flat in Kent. My other cats, as many of you will know, live in my lovely rural house in Cornwall and they are blissfully happy spending their days hunting, exploring and roaming freely. I always said I would never keep a cat indoors but when confronted with this poor little mite in need of the right home I couldn't refuse. I felt it would be a great way to experiment with all my environmental enrichment ideas to stimulate the bored house cat. Selfishly, I also felt that Mango (now called Mangus), the cat in question, would be great company whilst I bash away at my laptop . . . which she is. At first, I endeavoured to maintain control of the relationship and frequently ignored her when I was busy, encouraging her to be self-reliant. That worked for a while but I admit to letting my guard down (she is incredibly sweet). She saw the chink in my armour, went in for the kill and now rules the place completely. She takes up more of my bed than I do, dictates my every movement, and protests loudly, as anyone who telephones my office will testify, if I dare to stop tickling her whilst discussing a patient.

This is what we are up against. This is how they shape our

behaviour and we in turn shape theirs. I would like to think, with my experience, that I can see the warning signs and will never allow my relationship with Mangus to become dysfunctional. Sometimes when she looks at me I am not so sure . . .

Having experienced this epiphany about the true extent of the influence of our relationships with our cats, I want to pass the knowledge on. Understanding what is appropriate or inappropriate will potentially enhance your well-being and de-stress your cat. Accepting that cats are a different species with minimal social requirements and no fundamental need for a relationship of any sort is difficult since it flies in the face of everything we have ever believed about our unique bond with them. Whatever we specifically demand of them socially and emotionally, there must be something in the owner/cat bond that gives them pleasure too. I have absolutely no intention of destroying good, fun, happy kinships between cat and human. I am, however, suggesting that many of us, particularly if our cats are exhibiting problem behaviour, should review the relationship honestly and possibly tweak it a little before con-demning the cat.

I don't want this book to be full of warnings and foreboding about loving your cat too much. Half the fun of having cats is the fact that, if you are very lucky, they can be extraordinarily tolerant of stroking, squeezing and kissing. I would prefer to think of *Cat Counsellor* as a journey of discovery about what your cats want from you and from each other, and what you, fundamentally, want from them.

In order to truly understand the origins of the feline/human union I felt it was important to see how the relationship has grown over the centuries. The first chapter is therefore devoted to looking at a potted history of the domestic cat. I'm sure you've all heard much of it before: the cat as a deity in ancient Egypt in stark contrast with its vilification and persecution in the Middle Ages. Rather than dwell on the historical chronology, I want to explore the attitude of those people who worshipped or feared the cat to see if it sheds any light on our current obsession. I've also indulged myself by including a number of old cat superstitions and proverbs just to illustrate the significance of this tiny but enigmatic creature to many nations throughout the world.

In the subsequent two chapters I will focus on the cat's relationship with its own species. So many of us now keep more than one cat; this section of the book will show us how best to handle the stresses and strains of cohabitation for the fundamentally antisocial feline (they really aren't small dogs). And, although some of the problems you may experience are purely 'a cat thing', we are a nation of animal lovers and many of us embrace all species. Chapter 4 gives general advice about helping your cat to live harmoniously with all things furred and feathered. The rest of the book is devoted to exploring the complications of the human/cat relationship and how we should behave to get the best out of our cats. Most intriguing of all (I think) are Chapters 9 and 10, where I reveal the results of a national survey establishing why women find cats so incredibly alluring but also suggest a slightly controversial per-sonal theory that differs somewhat from the more traditional ideas. Definitely a voyage of discovery for me!

I haven't written *Cat Counsellor* as an instructional manual. It does contain advice on various subjects but there is no point going over ground that has been covered already by *Cat Confidential* and *Cat Detective*. Many of the stories in the chapters illustrate important points without actually offering solutions. Such is the nature of the beast that some problems are unfixable, however much of a pickle human beings get themselves into by trying. I hope that *Cat Counsellor* will give you a personal insight into what goes on in these special relationships. Whether you are a model with a moggy, a secretary with a Siamese or an artist with an Abyssinian I hope it helps you in some way to understand your cat better.

CHAPTER 1

A Love-Hate Relationship

EVERY DAY I EXPERIENCE EXAMPLES OF THE EXTRAORDINARY relationship that mankind has developed with the domestic cat. I marvel at the depth of my feelings for my own cats, Lucy, Annie, Bink and Mangus, and witness acts of incredible love and devotion during my typical working day as a cat behaviour counsellor. I have often suggested this to be a modern-day phenomenon, but in fact the human/cat bond has been around for thousands of years. We may currently express it differently in our insular western society but the allure of the feline is common to many races and has been for a very long time.

The origins of the relationship are probably best viewed by going back to ancient Egypt, circa 4000 BC, when cats were employed to keep mice and rats away from grain stores. For a long time this was considered to be the earliest reference to domestication, but a grave found in Cyprus in 1983, dating from 7500 BC, contained the skeletons of a human and a type of immature cat. Cats are not native to Cyprus so this discovery does rather suggest that cats were tamed or maybe even domesticated as early as that. Statues from Anatolia (the Asian part of Turkey) created around 6000 BC depict women playing with domesticated cats, so I have every suspicion that further evidence of a pre-Eygptian inter-species relationship is waiting to be uncovered. I doubt very much that cats were 'backward in coming forward' once they saw the obvious advantages of getting to know humans.

It is easy to see from history how the symbiotic nature of the human/cat relationship arose. Traditional nomadic lifestyles ceased so storage of crops was essential. The grain attracted quite a bit of interest from mice, rats and (inevitably) African wildcats. The cats were encouraged to stay around by the Egyptians, who fed them scraps by way of inducement. The presence of an abundance of food, both scavenged and caught, and the absence of predators or human deterrence meant that feline colonies soon formed.

All grain was stored in royal granaries, and as these large concentrations of goodies attracted huge quantities of mice it was essential that the Pharaoh had access to as many cats as possible to protect the precious commodity. It would have been extremely difficult to confiscate everyone's personal cats so in an obvious stroke of genius the Pharaoh made all cats demigods. A mere human couldn't own a demigod (only a god could do that) but they could look after them. Egyptians brought their fostered cats to work at the granary overnight and picked them up in the morning. For this service they received a tax credit and were able to claim their cats as dependents even though all cats were technically the property of the Pharaoh. It sounds great in theory but can you imagine taking your cat to work at the local granary and then picking him up again in the morning? For one thing, he would have left of his own accord before the whistle blew because he'd had enough; for another, as soon as he realized he was supposed to work with a bunch of other cats you wouldn't see him for dust; alternatively, you'd get him there once but never see him again as he'd immediately move in with someone more sympathetic. I cannot imagine how the system worked but it is well documented; were African wildcats so compliant? One thing is certain: the Egyptians would not have risked incurring the wrath of their Pharaoh so they were probably uniquely persistent.

The cats were always put first in the Egyptian household. After all, people were only human; cats were demigods. (Is it just me or is this equally true today?) When a cat died the family who housed it went into ritualistic mourning, shaving off their eyebrows and pounding their chests to show their grief at the loss. The cat's body was wrapped and brought to a priest to make sure the death was natural (killing or injuring a cat was a capital crime). It was then embalmed. Not surprisingly, people came to believe that cats had a direct influence on their health, and their fortunes.

Cats and religion

The ancient Egyptians regarded cats as embodiments of the fertility goddess Bast, also known as Bastet. Bastet was originally lion-headed, but she became depicted as a cat or a cat-headed woman as the appeal of the domestic cat grew. The ancient Egyptian symbol Ru (referring to, amongst other things, the symbolical transition from the spiritual plane to the material one) appeared in many magical texts at a time when cat and woman were worshipped as one and is shaped like the half-dilated pupil of a cat's eye. Egyptian art shows myriad images of cats in domestic situations, often sitting under the wife's chair to symbolize an enhancement of her fertility by association with Bastet. Cats were clearly doing what comes naturally, catching rodents and birds; humans were depicted as encouraging the behaviour or, at least, somehow facilitating it. Already the mighty cat had learnt the art of training humans.

It was not just the Egyptians who worshipped cats. The Roman goddess Diana, in her role as moon goddess, was linked with the cat and also with the feline-friendly number nine. Nine is a mystical number and can frequently be seen in various mythologies. It followed that Diana, long associated with the cat, should endow the animal with its proverbial nine lives. Freya, the Viking goddess of fertility, love and war, was strongly associated with cats also. Her chariot was driven by two large cats, Bygul and Trygul; and kittens were often given in her name to brides to ensure good fortune in love and romance.

The European faiths transferred many of the attributes of Bastet to their own deities, so the early Christian Church actively absorbed cult festivals. The Virgin Mary became the symbol of the virgin-mother goddess. The connection between the female and the cat even features in early Christian imagery, where a cat is seen giving birth in the manger where Mary cradled the baby Jesus. In a Leonardo da Vinci sketch of the Holy Family, Jesus is shown cradling a cat. The Copts, the original Christians in Egypt, believed that when the Holy Family fled to Egypt to escape Herod's infanticide they stayed for a while in Bubastis, where Bastet's temple was the centre of cat worship, at a time when the latter was at its height. In the Jewish Gospel of the Holy Twelve there is a tale of Jesus remonstrating with a crowd of ne'er-do-wells who were tormenting a cat; I'd like to think that He had a particular affection for felines!

The cat is highly respected in Islam because of tales that the prophet Muhammad was a cat lover. One story tells of a cat that saved Muhammad from being bitten by a deadly snake. In another tale, when Muhammad was called to prayer, his cat Muezza was asleep on the sleeve of his robe. Rather than disturb his cat, the prophet cut off the sleeve. He used water from which his cat had drunk to wash himself and his wife ate from the dish from which Muezza had eaten, such was their devotion.

In Burma and Siam people believed that the souls of the departed lived in the bodies of cats before moving on to the next life. In Japan religious ceremonies were held for the souls of departed cats. According to Chinese myth cats were supernatural creatures who could detect ghosts and evil spirits; the cat god, Li Shou, is said to ward off evil spirits of the night. Agricultural deities in China were also often depicted in the form of cats. It is hard to find a culture or religion without references to cats as symbols of fertility, wisdom, protection or good fortune.

All the great cat goddesses such as Bastet and Diana, with their link to the moon, combine both feminine and feline attributes. Since time immemorial, women have been thought to possess the ability to be mediums, soothsayers and clairvoyants. Intuition too is deemed to be a female attribute. Cats have an enigmatic quality that makes them appear wise and 'knowing'. They are often described as 'old souls' – I've done so myself – and the attraction of women to cats could be seen to represent a link to an ancient part of the human soul. This may seem fanciful but thousands of years of cat history, myths and legends amount to a powerful influence on modern-day thinking. Any animal that has been the subject of a massive swing in human reaction from deification to persecution to deification again (we do worship them, let's face it) in the space of a few thousand years must be fairly special. Even today, when the domestic cat is experiencing unprecedented popularity as a pet in the western world, people seem to be divided between cat lovers and cat haters. Such is the influence of Sooty, Ginger and Tigger that there appear to be very few fence-sitters.

Cats spread throughout the world

Cats were routinely kept on ships for rodent control and viewed as important members of the crew (even Nelson had a cat called Tiddles who saw quite a bit of nautical action before dying in battle). There are numerous stories of heroic cats including that of Able Seaman Simon, a black and white moggy who was badly injured on the Royal Navy frigate HMS *Amethyst* in 1949. He was treated along with the injured sailors and, as he recovered, he patrolled the sick ward and gave comfort to the men. He was promoted to Able Seaman for his services to morale. Sadly he died in quarantine when he got back home but it was he who received the most media attention upon his return to Plymouth.

In the early days, it wasn't long before journeys across the Mediterranean enabled cats to populate other continents and, you might be forgiven for thinking, start their strategic planning for world domination. Wherever they arrived they were obviously received with good grace; they performed a useful role in vermin control but also became willing pets and companions. By the fourth century AD word of the cat's usefulness as a rodent deterrent had spread throughout the Roman Empire, whose occupation of much of Europe and parts of North Africa and the Middle East enabled more homes to play host to the domestic cat. In the 1700s cats were imported into the New World from Europe when colonies of settlers were overcome by plagues of rats, and they charmed yet another continent into permanent cohabitation. Rodent eradication was undoubtedly the initial key to their success but there are clues everywhere to show that their predatory skills were only half the story.

Cats in art

Art is a useful indicator in the exploration of social history, and early paintings and pottery from Greece, Rome, China and Japan, for example, depict children playing with pet cats in their homes. A mosaic panel dating from Roman times in the Naples museum shows a domestic tabby cat with its paw on a bird ready to devour it. Small cats kept as household pets appear on works of Greek art of the fifth and fourth centuries BC. Silver coins show naked youths playing with, or accompanied by, tiny felines. Several versions show the cat leaping for a bird held in the boy's hand or pouncing in pursuit of a ball. House cats are portrayed playing with balls of wool on vases in the British Museum. The Chinese and Japanese depicted the cat in delicate watercolours; clearly indicating that the cat was important in the oriental way of life also. The air of equanimity which surrounded the cat and its aura of inner wisdom were qualities with which Buddhists could empathize. Many compositions in ancient art include a toy, so I am sure my obsession with a fishing-rod contraption with a feather on the end is hardly new. It is interesting to see that the cat's early role in human society consisted of what comes naturally: hunting prey. There was no manipulation through selective breeding to change the status quo. All that man succeeded in doing was enabling the cat to see the obvious advantages of human dwellings and the entertainment value of the inhabitants. We have been at their beck and call ever since; clever animals!

The persecution of the cat

Unfortunately there was a period in history when cats didn't get their own way. They had for centuries been revered for their apparently supernatural abilities, and their tendency to be rather independent further accentuated that air of mystery. However, as time went on they developed a more cultish status and came to be associated with various religious rituals. In medieval France cats were sacrificed to ensure a successful harvest, and were seen as the familiars of witches. The Catholic Church demonized cats in the thirteenth century when their association with the pagan goddess Freya led them to be regarded as the manifestation of the devil. Hundreds of thousands of cats were tortured, burned at the stake or roasted alive and cat numbers plummeted by over 90 per cent. The cat population was also affected by the plague, as they were erroneously blamed for carrying the disease and therefore culled on sight. Ironically, when so many humans were dying from the plague that there was no-one to spare to cull the cats, they were able to kill the rats *truly* responsible for the spread of the disease.

However, even during this darkest period in their history, there were still people who loved and cherished cats. Many farmers would not give up their cats because of their obvious contribution to pest control; and there must have been countless old women (in the Middle Ages this category would have included anyone over the age of forty) who, ignored by a male-orientated society that had no further use for them, lonely and isolated while the younger family members were working, would turn to the company of a hungry feral cat, thus reinforcing the popular association between the 'witch' and her cats originally suggested by the historical and religious woman/feline link. Unfortunately, if any misfortunes occurred, old women were often blamed, together with their cats, who were seen as willing accomplices. I just thank goodness I wasn't around at the time. The finger of suspicion would undoubtedly have pointed at me!

Cats continued to be ritualistically slaughtered or casually tortured well into the nineteenth century in various parts of Europe. Unlike dogs, cats were seen as elusive, independent and highly resistant to human influence and domination. In a male-orientated society it would not have been appropriate to consort with an animal with such a 'feminine' quality; it would surely render any man susceptible to the charge of weakness and – by extension – impotence. In the circumstances I am amazed that the cat ever made a comeback.

It is extremely hard to understand the mentality of humans at a time when an animal's life was considered worthless. We are blessed with a society now that largely abhors cruelty to any living creature and many people will campaign tirelessly for their welfare. However, I think it's important to remember that in those days mere survival was still the key motivation. There can have been little room left for compassion for animals if those animals did not represent livelihoods and food. In twenty-first-century Britain we take subsistence for granted and pursue other things instead: happiness maybe, or entertainment, or material possessions. It is far easier for us to spare a thought for animals; our very survival is no longer uppermost in our minds.

The revival of the cat

Such is the nature and influence of the cat, however, that make a comeback it did. It was reluctantly agreed that cats had helped to reduce the spread of the plague and they began to creep back into favour, but this process was not fully established until well into the nineteenth century, when the Christian churches finally stopped persecuting 'witches' and their familiars. Attitudes towards animals in general became more caring and in 1824 the Society for the Prevention of Cruelty to Animals was founded, later given the royal seal of approval by Queen Victoria in 1840. The expansion of towns and cities in Britain meant that feral cats far out-numbered the house variety in Victorian times. The mood of the nation was changing, however, as I have said, and in 1871 the first cat show took place; the organizer's aim was to encourage public perception of the cat as a household pet. By 1887 the first national cat club of Great Britain was established and the cat has gone from strength to strength ever since. In 1927 the Cats' Protection League was founded, solely to promote the welfare of cats in the UK.

Initially the intention of Harrison Weir, the organizer of the first cat show, was also to promote the care and welfare of the cat. He had seen the neglect and abuse that they had been subjected to and, as a genuine cat lover, he wanted to publicize their true nature and educate people away from their ill-treatment. Sadly he gave up judging at cat shows twenty-one years later because he was disillusioned about the results of his efforts. He felt that the breeders and members of the cat club were more interested in winning prizes than in promoting cat welfare. In *Cats And All About Them*, a book written by a breeder of Persians (Frances Simpson) in 1902, it is quite apparent that her good-natured advice is geared towards encouraging cat fanciers to breed for both pleasure and profit. (Seeing old photographs of pedigrees does focus the mind on the current obsession with extremes; the breeds of one hundred years ago are merely gentle variations on nature's own perfect specimen.) Throughout this book and others of its time it is clear that 'cat lovers' are people with a living, breathing hobby whose ultimate aim is to forge friendships with other 'cat lovers' and win prizes, just as Harrison Weir lamented. The enthusiasts of this era obviously had an interest in cats but they were, after all, only cats.

Leaping forward to publications of the 1960s (my first decade on this planet and therefore my own first personal experience of the human/cat relationship) we find that there is a distinct change in mood. There is a constant sense of anthropomorphism and interpretation of behaviour in a very human context. It is clear that the 'pet' part of the relationship is changing subtly into something more emotional. In one publication called *Cats' ABC* by Beverley Nichols, for example, there is an interesting subtext that shows a strong regard for 'feline people' and a dismissive snarl at all those guilty of a 'non-feline' persuasion. These 'us' and 'them' camps are still very much in evidence today.

In my opinion cinema and television have played a major role in changing our perception of the nature of the cat. They may just have been reflecting the mood and beliefs of the time but they are certainly significant in reinforcing our perceptions. Cartoon characters such as Felix the Cat, Tom and Jerry, Sylvester and Tweety Pie, Top Cat and Garfield show cats that exhibit human traits. Many even talk, whilst still retaining feline characteristics. Are these cartoons and similar representations guilty of creating an imaginary concept of the human/cat hybrid that is buried somewhere in our subconscious? Johnny Morris (a great hero of mine) has a lot to answer for when it comes to giving a voice to animals. The 1960s children's programme *Animal Magic* showed him as the zookeeper discussing various species and, undoubtedly to make the information more accessible, providing a 'voice-over' of the animals talking back and joining in the narrative. *Animal Magic* obviously got to me as, in 'conversations' with cats, I will often give my own verbal interpretation of what they are saying using a form of primitive ventriloquism, just as Johnny did. This has amused many of the vets and nurses I have worked with over the years, but it is easy to see how you might start to believe that cats are capable of complex reasoning. They really are *not* small people in zip-up furry coats. I think it is just as easy (and better for them) to love cats for being cats.

So our quick overview of the historical background to our relationship with our cats has reached the present day. Books about cats now have titles such as *Yoga for Cats*, *Psycho Pussy* and *Do Cats Need Shrinks?* We board our pets in hotels when we go away on holiday and carry their photograph to show anyone who is interested. Cat ownership is a multi-million-pound business; we spend a fortune on medical bills, toys, food and videos to entertain them when we are out. It is even technically possible to make a diamond out of the cremated ashes of our dearly departed cat or clone them using their DNA as the ultimate memorial. However, just before we get down to the brass tacks of cat relationships and how to survive them, here is a plethora of trivia!

Famous ailurophiles (cat lovers)

As if we didn't know already, there have been many famous and noteworthy cat lovers including Sir Winston Churchill, Abraham Lincoln, Charles Dickens, Theodore Roosevelt, Ronald Reagan, Nostradamus, the Duke of Wellington, Queen Victoria, Sir Isaac Newton, Florence Nightingale, Beatrix Potter, Sir Walter Scott, Renoir, Monet, William Wordsworth, Horatio Nelson, Thomas Hardy, Victor Hugo . . . (an impressive list, I'm sure you will agree) and more recently Bill Clinton, Halle Berry, Billy Crystal, Warren Beatty, Yoko Ono, Rolf Harris, Ann Widdecombe MP, the Osbournes, Ricky Gervais, Jonathan Ross . . .

Interestingly, famous ailurophobes (cat haters) include Napoleon, Mussolini, Hitler and Genghis Khan . . . need I say more?

To further enhance the story of the significance of the cat in just about every nation's culture there are numerous superstitions and proverbs bestowing incredible powers to our feline friends.

Superstitions from around the world

- A tabby cat is considered lucky, especially if it takes up residence in your home of its own accord. This is a sign that money is coming to you.
- The British believe that if a black cat crosses your path, good luck follows; Americans believe that it is bad luck.
- Touching a cat causes loss of memory.
- A cat sneezing is a good omen for everyone who hears it.
- A three-coloured cat will keep the house safe from fire.
- If you dream of a tortoiseshell you will be lucky in love.
- If you dream of two cats fighting it foretells illness or a quarrel.
- If you kick a cat, you will develop rheumatism in that leg.
- Letting a cat look into a mirror will cause you trouble.
- On every black cat there is a single white hair which will bring wealth or love to the person who removes it without the cat's scratching them (don't try this at home).

Proverbs from around the world
- In a cat's eyes all things belong to cats – England
- Beware of people who dislike cats – Ireland
- All cats are bad in May – France
- After dark all cats are leopards – New Mexico
- I gave an order to a cat and the cat gave it to its tail – China
- You will always be lucky if you know how to make friends with strange cats – Colonial America
- Happy is the home with at least one cat – Italy

- The cat's a saint when there are no mice about – Japan
- If you play with a cat you must not mind her scratch – Yiddish origin

I would like to think that I have put a good case forward for the cat although I feel I am probably preaching to the converted. They are now populating our homes by the millions and, almost without exception, are an important member of the family. The fact that 'the family' is no longer an exclusive club for humans can have quite far-reaching implications. In order to be a social unit in the proper sense we have to understand the nature of cat relationships to make it work to the benefit of everyone. That's only fair.

CHAPTER 2

Can Cats Share?

I SPEND A LOT OF TIME TELLING PEOPLE THAT MULTI-CAT households don't work, but I think it's important to recognize that there is another perspective. I work with cats that don't get on; without exception the problems I see in multi-cat households are related to overcrowding in the house or the territory. For some cats two is a crowd so I can't even blame owners for unreasonable cat acquisition (here speaks a woman who has lived with seven); this really is a cat thing. However, for many cats, living with a feline companion is reassuring and entertaining and the exchanges between them look, to all intents and purposes, like genuine affection. For example, my friend's cats Whiskey, George and Lady have been together for many years. Only the other day I visited to find Whiskey and

George curled up together in an impossibly small cat basket with their paws entwined round each other's bodies. Every now and then George washed Whiskey and Whiskey washed George and then both settled down with contented sighs to sleep in each other's embrace. They share a litter tray, food bowls, laps and beds and demonstrate the perfect example of domestic bliss. It's very unlike the behaviour of the cats I spend my working life with but probably a common scenario in many lucky households throughout the land. It was only when all three cats collectively jumped when the cat flap rattled that I realized their sociable natures hid the innate suspicion of others that dwells within all domestic felines to some degree.

Whatever relationships are forged within the home (or even with Tigger next door) it is no coincidence that so many cats are behaving badly and developing stress-related illnesses. There are a lot of cats in some areas and this spells trouble for the average moggy stuck in the middle of so many overlapping territories. Many of the cats I visit live in places chosen specifically for them. Owners seek out cul-de-sacs, unmade roads and quiet streets in order that their cherished pets do not fall victim to speeding cars. However, all the neighbours in this cat-friendly haven had exactly the same idea. Therefore, what you end up with is a bunch of cats (without a fractured pelvis between them) putting each other through hell fighting for rights of passage in a vastly overcrowded territory. How ironic that our best intentions can have such a disastrous effect.

The next few case histories illustrate some of the potential pitfalls of a multi-cat household. The first two stories in this chapter discuss the most potentially difficult social dilemma – introducing number two cat to number one. Single cats may look lonely and bereft of feline company but the truth is often quite different. Any socializing that the cat might crave can be satisfied by a quick foray into the garden next door for some eyeballing with the ginger tom. If you are really fortunate the interaction may involve a quick game, a little mutual grooming and various other pleasant activities. Do not, however, be fooled into believing that this obvious kinship would be quite so evident if the ginger tom came through your cat flap; certain things are sacrosanct. The two cases I illustrate here did not stem from any conscious effort by either owner to provide company; the situation was thrust upon them as something of a fait accompli. Nevertheless, if you decide that your cat is genuinely lonely when you are out at work and you cannot resist adding to your feline family then there is advice below that may limit the risk of a complete disaster.

Paddy and Butch – the cats that put an end to the ironing

There is nothing worse than having a cat fight in the tranquil surroundings of your own home. My great friend and colleague Robin Walker refers to this as 'the war on the living-room floor' and he couldn't be more accurate in his description. Whenever this happens there is an enormous temptation to intervene. We want to punish, we want to console and generally get involved in something that is, fundamentally, a cat thing. How many times have you sat stroking one of your cats whilst contorting yourself in an attempt to give attention to the other one at the same time to avoid jealousy? How many times have you plunged into the middle of your two cats to remove the aggressor? Trust me, avoid pulled muscles and ripped flesh in the future. It doesn't work like that. Paddy's and Butch's owners found this out the hard way.

Sally and Megan were sisters. They had both divorced within a couple of years of each other and decided that living alone in two properties just didn't make any economic sense. They had always been great friends so decided to pool their resources and buy a house together. Sally had an eight-year-old tabby moggy called Butch and Megan had an ex-stray of indeterminate age called Paddy. They each knew and loved the other's cat so it didn't really occur to them that Paddy and Butch wouldn't feel the same. Of course they would get on. The day of the move came and Sally and Butch arrived first, closely followed by Megan's furniture and then her cat. The sisters decided, once settled, that the best idea would be to let the cats out in the living room and allow them to explore and get to know each other. Both cat baskets were opened at the agreed time at opposite ends of the room and Sally and Megan sat back to witness the introduction. Paddy and Butch stared at each other with low rumbling growls and the occasional hiss for good measure from the safety of their cat carriers. Just as Megan was about to say 'Oh well, it could be worse', Butch launched himself like a rocket at Paddy's basket. At the same moment Paddy threw himself sideways and disappeared behind the sofa to avoid the imminent attack. Sally and Megan each screamed 'NO' and instinctively rushed to her own cat to administer whatever reassurance was necessary to prevent bloodshed. Unfortunately it's difficult to reason with a cat consumed with evil intent and both Sally and Megan became fearful for their own safety. The fight continued but eventually, with the aid of a chair and a large cardboard box, Butch was steered into the kitchen and the door shut behind him. Paddy was retrieved from the bottom of the television cabinet where he had sought refuge.

Sally and Megan were in a tearful state of shock. How could

this have happened? How could they have totally failed to predict their cats' behaviour? I got the call some weeks later after they had spoken to their vet. The long days since their move had been difficult. Both Sally and Megan had spent all their time at home following the cats around in a low crouch with outstretched arms to herd them about the house and prevent fights. Occasionally they were not vigilant enough and the two cats met nose to nose. Paddy would usually spit in Butch's face and that would start the fur flying. Megan and Sally would then rush from their respective locations and dive into the fray. Sally had already sustained some painful scratches to her head during one of these rugby tackles.

Both cats had previously lived alone and obviously thoroughly enjoyed it. Butch had always been territorial in his garden and surrounding area but a soft teddy bear at home. He wasn't quite so cuddly when I saw him as he clearly knew Paddy was nearby and ripe for a good squashing. His brow was furrowed, he was rather tense and he didn't like being confined or the atmosphere in the house. Paddy had also enjoyed life as a singleton, but only for the past couple of years. Prior to that it was anyone's guess what he had endured. He might have been wrong-footed when Butch launched his pre-emptive strike but I was sure that, given a little more warning next time, he would be equally keen to establish his own set of rights.

I listened to the sisters explaining how they were very proactive in their cats' disputes. Every move they made was governed by the behaviour of their cats. For example, Paddy felt safer in a high place so every time Megan got the ironing board out he would jump on top before she even switched the iron on. Needless to say both sisters' clothes were looking a little creased; nothing was getting ironed. They also spoke in urgent whispers and moved around the house in quiet slow motion; the air just reeked of tension. I soon found myself whispering too, it was so contagious. This had to stop!

I explained to Sally and Megan that pussy-footing and whispering weren't conducive to a relaxed environment. All their actions, despite their intentions, were fuelling the fires of hatred between Butch and Paddy. The cats were sensing their owners' anxiety and feeling justified in their perception of threat and danger. After all, if Sally and Megan were that scared then the cats had every right to be on red alert.

We devised a battle plan that would take the heat out of the situation. I didn't want to make the proposed therapy programme too structured or formal; I rather hoped that changing the way Sally and Megan behaved would have a big enough impact. I had a strong sense that the fighting was motivated to a large extent by the atmosphere of tension in the home. I asked Sally and Megan to create some new areas indoors purely for the cats: shelving to allow them to view each other from high vantage points and secret private areas for escape and time out. This would enable Paddy to use structures other than the ironing board to get away from Butch and both cats would benefit from rest in secluded places where they felt they were out of danger. The most important part of the programme involved changing Sally and Megan's behaviour. I asked them to stop worrying and start relaxing. I tried to convince them that the fighting would cease if they chilled out. No more refereeing or furtive whispering; bring on the yoga and whale song.

A series of emails ensued that detailed the progress made over the next few weeks. My hunch was right and almost immediately Sally and Megan saw the results of their new-found calm. After the first five days of little or no response to their cats' altercations Sally noticed that Butch and Paddy touched noses without serious repercussions. This was indeed a triumph and it encouraged them to continue with their policy of ignoring the cats whilst appearing incredibly relaxed. It took their pussy pugilists a while to discover the network of shelving throughout the house but the secret hideaways under the bed and in the cupboard were found immediately and used regularly. By the end of the eight-week period Sally and Megan had become almost cocky, wondering what all the fuss had been about. Butch and Paddy were not exactly bosom buddies (I never promised that) but they seemed to have agreed to disagree. They would still scrap, growl and hiss at each other from time to time but the most this elicited from Sally or Megan would be the rather gentle reprimand of 'Language, Butch/Paddy!'

It was great to be able to turn the corner for Butch and Paddy by changing the owners' behaviour but it isn't always that straightforward. Most human intervention will make things worse but there are often measures that can be taken environmentally that will also reap rewards.

Chloe and Lay-by Laddie – the marriage made in hell

Throughout my working life I get to meet the most extraordinary people but some really stick in my mind. It could be because they are particularly charming or conscientious with their behaviour programme or just plain barking. However, Bill and Irene will always have a place in my heart as probably the most stubborn, determined and kind-natured couple you could ever wish to meet. They also have the dubious honour of being part of the longest behaviour therapy programme I have ever undertaken. Let me explain why.

Bill was a long-distance lorry driver and he spent many days away from home. During one of his stints 'up north' he found himself on a dual carriageway in need of a rest. As he scanned the road for suitable parking he passed a small lay-by. He had already dismissed it as too small for his artic but something about the rough piece of ground made him look twice. There, sitting on the edge of the busy main road, was a scruffy black cat, his fur rippling and his little body leaning back with the force of each juggernaut as it thundered past. Bill was confused; he'd seen many cats sitting on verges but they were always focusing on some poor rodent in a hedge. Surely this one wasn't planning to cross the road? Bill was a great cat lover; he even had a picture of his beloved tortoiseshell, Chloe, in his cab (and one of his wife, Irene, of course). He couldn't possibly drive on without checking that the little black cat was safe. He soon found a large parking area and left his truck to return to the lay-by. He fully expected the black cat to be gone or flattened but, to his great relief, the little fellow was still sitting by the side of the road being blown about by the traffic. As Bill approached he started to talk softly to the cat and crouch down; he didn't want to scare him into the path of a speeding car. The cat remained still and watched Bill as he crept towards him. Suddenly Bill realized that the little black cat wasn't right at all. He was sitting upright, but awkwardly, and as he moved towards Bill's outstretched hand to sniff his fingers he dragged himself forward by his front legs without getting up. Bill knew immediately that the cat was injured and probably paralysed. He removed his jacket and very carefully placed the little black cat in this makeshift stretcher and carried him back to the lorry. A few phone calls later Bill was making a detour to the local veterinary surgery where they awaited his arrival. As Bill drove he was moved to see the little black cat lying next to him, purring and gazing into his eyes. He promised him that everything would be done to fix him and make him more comfortable.

Six weeks and £2000 later little 'Lay-by Laddie' was recovering well. He had suffered a fractured pelvis and broken leg; the vet was amazed at his resilience since it was clear the injuries had been sustained some days before his meeting with Bill. During his extensive hospital treatment Bill had returned home to Irene and Chloe but he monitored Lay-by Laddie's progress on a daily basis and always visited him when he was driving in that part of the country. He also paid the extensive bills without a second thought as no owner had been found, so it was evident where Laddie would be going once he was back on his feet.

Chloe, a delicate tortoiseshell and white cat, had always been rather shy and retiring. Irene and Bill loved her dearly but the relationship felt a little one-sided. They spoke to her, they stroked her, they gave her all the love she could possibly want but she remained steadfastly under the bed or in the wardrobe 90 per cent of the time. How wonderful it would be for her to have a companion, they mused, who might just bring her out of herself. Secretly they both admitted that bringing Lay-by Laddie home was just as much about their needs as about Chloe's. With a little tender loving care, castration and a lot of good food he had become a handsome and affectionate cat, charming all the nurses at the vet's surgery and winning Bill over completely. He was definitely going to be the sort of cat who would take any amount of hugging and squeezing. So, with a little bag of goodies from the staff, he left the hospital to start the journey to his new home.

Bill and Irene knew that it was important to make a gentle introduction between the two cats. They were not overly concerned as they felt sure Chloe would welcome Lay-by Laddie with open paws once she saw what a little charmer he was. When he got home he was placed in the dining room with his own bed, litter tray, food and water and a selection of toys. This would be his den for a couple of days until it was time to 'meet and greet' his new companion.

That weekend they decided to let Lay-by Laddie out of the dining room to explore the rest of the house. Chloe had already shown some interest in him by sniffing under the door but she always walked away looking seriously unfazed. It was bound to be fine. As he took his first steps out into the hallway, Chloe watched casually from the worktop in the kitchen. Lay-by Laddie sauntered past her and drank a little water from her bowl before sitting down under the kitchen table and washing his paw. Domestic bliss; all was apparently well. For the next three days the two cats cohabited without any friction, and then came Tuesday morning. Chloe was sitting once again on the work surface in the kitchen as Irene opened a tin of cat food for their breakfast. Lay-by Laddie heard the telltale sound of impending grub and rushed into the kitchen with great excitement. Chloe was spooked and jumped backwards off the worktop; Lay-by Laddie then decided (rather ill-advisedly) to bash her round the head for her trouble. Chloe screamed and retreated upstairs followed by Lay-by Laddie followed by Irene. A huge storm of flying fur later Lay-by Laddie was once more confined to the dining room and Chloe was being comforted by a rather stressed owner. It was soon apparent that things had gone disastrously wrong. Lay-by Laddie and Chloe could not be left alone together. He wasn't fighting with her or bullying her every time; sometimes he wasn't doing anything more than looking at her. She would see him, get the screaming ab-dabs and rush under the bed for the rest of the day. He could almost be seen sniggering as he wound round his owners' legs: 'What'd I say? What'd I do?' This was not a marriage made in heaven.

Bill and Irene realized that a stalemate had been reached and they called me for help. I listened to their story and, when I visited, I was also bowled over by Lay-by Laddie's cute nature and gentle ways. However, I wasn't fooled. Here was that typical case of entire (in Lay-by-Laddie's case recently entire) stray tomcat (very affectionate) being adopted and moving in with the resident cat. All is well for a while as he susses the opposition and then, WHAM! He sees that the other cat is a wimp and all he has to do is look in her general direction to bring about complete disintegration. She dissolves in a heap and the tomcat takes over her home whilst, every now and then, beating her up mercilessly just to prove a point. Sadly, Lay-by Laddie had adopted this strategy and poor Chloe was absolutely terrified. By the time I visited she hadn't come downstairs for ten days.

There are occasions when, with the best will in the world, some cats should not be kept together. I listened to Bill's story and I listened to Irene's concerns and I found it hard to say anything constructive or positive about the future for Lay-by Laddie and Chloe as an item. However, I can never just walk away from even the worst scenario with an 'Oops, sorry, can't help you' (unless of course it involves seven cats from Singapore; more of that later) so I discussed a plan of gradual reintroduction for Chloe and Lay-by Laddie. I asked Bill to construct a wooden frame covered with chicken wire that would fit inside a doorway, working on the principle that the cats should have sight and smell of each other before allowing direct contact.

We also ensured the home had plenty of cat goodies around to avoid the need for competition. Lay-by Laddie would be given access to the house on a timeshare basis with Chloe safely ensconced behind the chicken wire frame in her favourite bedroom hideaway. On alternate occasions Lay-by Laddie would be in the dining room (now definitely his domain) and Chloe would venture forth and stretch her legs. Every few weeks Irene and Bill attempted to mix them and each time it ended in tears.

After eight weeks I had to talk seriously to Bill and Irene about the future. It wasn't working and they had two seriously fed-up pussies on their hands. Would they consider finding a lovely new home for Lay-by Laddie? The answer was, not surprisingly, a resounding no. It had to work. So that is how I embarked on the longest behaviour therapy programme known to man. We persevered and maintained the exposure without direct contact whilst rotating the cats through various rooms. Lay-by Laddie was introduced to the garden and both cats enjoyed timeshare out there too. Every week over the next nine months Irene phoned to give me a progress report. I was astonished by her resilience. Bill was often away driving his truck and the full responsibility fell on her shoulders most of the time, but she didn't give up. She didn't even falter.

During the ninth month something happened. It appeared that Irene and Bill had at last broken Lay-by Laddie's resolve. He seemed to breathe a huge sigh of resignation and reluctantly agree to disagree. Chloe, on seeing that her adversary had become passive, returned to her normal everyday existence. She stayed under the bed and he stayed in the dining room or rubbed round Irene's legs. The chicken-wire frame was taken down and peace reigned at last. I missed those phone calls so I was delighted to hear from Irene and Bill some months later. Tragically the news wasn't good. Lay-by Laddie had gone out one day and not returned. He never seemed to venture much further than the garden but, for some reason, he didn't come in for his tea that night and was never seen again. They contacted rescue catteries, vet surgeries, the council, put up posters, but all to no avail. He had been gone ten days when they called me and is still missing to this day. It is tragic when things like this happen; there is nothing worse than losing a cat in this way without any understanding of their fate. It seemed particularly sad for Irene and Bill, given their determination to make things work for Chloe and Lay-by Laddie. I'd like to think that somebody somewhere is currently benefiting from his company.

Rhubarb and Hazel – the day the volcano erupted

Many cat households exist in an atmosphere of rumbling discontent that is difficult for owners to appreciate without knowing what to look for. It is easy to presume that all is well if there is no fighting. However, tension between cats can simmer like an active volcano and any sudden trauma or challenge can cause a massive eruption. Anxiety and stress reach fever pitch and previously tolerable relationships can be broken for ever.

This next case was a first for me: the only time I have left a consultation taking the patient with me. It also has a claim to fame as the case about which I wrote the fewest notes (five sentences to be exact). However, I remember it all as if it were yesterday. It started with yet another tearful and distressed telephone call early one morning. Elizabeth was distraught: one of her cats, Hazel, had visited the vet two days ago for dental treatment. When she was brought home that evening she had been attacked viciously by her companion, Rhubarb. Elizabeth was deeply shocked by this and the next two days had been a nightmare. Hazel was shut in a tiny room and whenever Elizabeth had let her out *she* had attacked Rhubarb! They were now permanently separated and Elizabeth was a shadow of her former self; she desperately needed help to return things to normal. I had seen many cases of this kind. Two cats live together but feel little if any genuine affection for each other. One goes to the vet, comes back smelling different, and an attack is launched. All their previous pent-up emotions and social issues come to the fore and they can never return to normality again; a genuine irretrievable breakdown of a relationship that was dodgy in the first place. I had an idea that I would be merely consoling Elizabeth and recommending she rehomed one of her cats.

I reserved judgement but didn't expect to find such a dreadful situation. Elizabeth lived alone in a two-bedroom (rather cramped) maisonette. She kept Rhubarb and Hazel indoors because she was frightened of losing them. She went out to work all day and the cats were left to their own devices. She didn't allow them in her bedroom so they had the run of a small sitting room, kitchenette, hallway, stairs and boxroom upstairs. When she was at home they were with her all the time, crying and looking for attention. This was their life and Elizabeth couldn't see anything wrong with it whatsoever; they were loved and that was all that mattered. After all, they seemed happy enough. When I visited, Hazel was shut into the box-room (I could hear her scratching at the door and crying). Rhubarb was behind the sofa, peering out from time to time looking rather forlorn. After some discussion with Elizabeth I decided to attempt a controlled meeting between the two cats. Elizabeth was borderline hysterical at this point but I reassured her that all would be well; I had to see the extent of their emotional response. (Can I just say that this was a lesson well learnt for me: namely, if the owner is against such exposure between two cats, don't do it!)

Elizabeth reluctantly collected Hazel from the boxroom and carried her downstairs. I sat on the floor, in between the door and Rhubarb's hiding place, armed with a tapestry cushion. Elizabeth put Hazel down in the hallway and as she burst into the room I remember wishing I had armed myself with something a little more robust. She immediately wailed like a banshee and launched herself in the direction of Rhubarb, who had been peering round the edge of the sofa in sheer terror. He immediately ran round to emerge from the other side of the sofa as Hazel did a quick change of direction and I fell flat on my face having rugby tackled the speeding aggressor and missed. A major scuffle followed as the two cats connected and their screaming was only surpassed by that of Elizabeth. I had completely lost my dignity at this stage and my only mission was to stop the fighting and pray that neither cat was injured. I plunged into the fray armed only with panic and the tapestry cushion (don't try this at home) and managed to scruff Rhubarb and pull him away. I rushed into the hallway, slammed the door and released a very shaken Rhubarb with a stroke and profuse apology. He immediately disappeared into the depths of the boxroom, not to be seen again that evening.

I returned to the sitting room, having regained a degree of composure, and sat down with Elizabeth to discuss what to do next. One good thing that came from this unfortunate encounter was an understanding that there was no way forward for Elizabeth. She told me that she was suffering from depression, anxiety and stress, and was on constant medication. She could not bear to cope with this situation for another moment so one of the cats had to leave. I totally agreed with her but probably for other reasons. These cats were confined in a small and non-stimulating environment. Their proximity was causing some distress but fighting had previously not been an option because of the lack of availability of escape routes. Where could either cat go when retreating? There was nowhere to hide but the tension between them was growing. The sudden adrenalin rush that occurred when Hazel returned from the vet's surgery was the trigger to attack in a 'kill or be killed' response to imminent danger. It was probably as excited and intensely emotional as either cat had ever been and they had become destined to repeat the behaviour as a dramatic release of all their pent-up frustrations. I would have been delighted if she had agreed to rehome *both* the cats.

After several hours Elizabeth agreed that Hazel would have to go. She was the less nervous and clingy of the two cats and more likely to appeal to a new owner. Once Elizabeth had decided to give up her pet she wasn't prepared to wait. Her emotions were at fever pitch and she pleaded with me to take the cat there and then. I very reluctantly made a call to her vet and they agreed to take her in that night and attempt to find a new home for her. I left that house taking the patient with me. I thought the only lesson to be learnt from this experience was that keeping cats indoors in a cramped and confined environment without any appropriate stimulation was a recipe for disaster. Any perceived danger would potentially lead to this sort of aggression and any tolerable relationship would be destroyed. I was wrong; that wasn't the only lesson I learnt. I had a phone call from the vet the following day to say that they had heard from Elizabeth. She wanted Hazel back; she had decided to keep her but asked the vet to put Rhubarb to sleep because it wouldn't be fair to rehome him because he was so shy. I wrote to Elizabeth and left a message for her to contact me but she never returned my call. I didn't pursue the matter. It is too easy for pet behaviour counsellors to become emotionally involved in every case, which can only be to the detriment of their own health and that of future patients. I know the veterinary practice involved and I am sure they would have used all their persuasive skills to reassure Elizabeth that there was a future for Rhubarb. I would like to think of him sunning himself somewhere in a small garden without a care in the world. I hope Hazel and Elizabeth are happy too.

❖   ❖   ❖

I see several cases of redirected aggression of this kind every year; I give advice on many others over the telephone. The problem always seems more intense and intractable in households where the cats are kept exclusively indoors like Hazel and Rhubarb. In my experience the most serious scenarios involve two cats only, shortly after the onset of social maturity (around the age of two). If, however, the cats have lived together without too much grief for six or seven years you have a sporting chance of getting things back to normal. This next case will give you some ideas if you are experiencing a similar dilemma.

Buttons and Beau – the battling Birman brothers and the broken bones

Katie left several messages on my answerphone in the office in the space of four hours; I realized things were obviously urgent when I returned her call that evening. The most dreadful thing had happened and it had left her reeling. It had also put her in hospital. She proceeded to explain. Buttons and Beau were eight-year-old brothers, gorgeous Birmans, and Katie was besotted with them. They had been adopted four years previously from a local sanctuary where they had found them-selves after a marriage breakdown. They lived with Katie and her husband Phil as indoor cats. After careful consideration Katie felt their coats were too high-maintenance to justify sending them out into an environment full of mud, slugs and twigs.

They had lived in harmony (allegedly) until four days ago, when the dreadful thing happened. Buttons hadn't been too well recently and the vet had diagnosed laryngitis. Shortly afterwards there had been a fight on the landing between the brothers, centred round the water bowl that was traditionally located there. Beau hadn't been looking himself either recently and a visit to the vet the following day confirmed that he too had succumbed to the same infection. When Katie brought Beau home that morning she was not prepared for the night-mare that ensued. She put the cat carrier down in the hallway and opened it as Buttons came sniffing towards Beau to investigate all the challenging smells his brother had brought home with him. Katie expected a 'Phew, it's great to be home' sort of reaction from Beau but instead he launched himself out of the cat basket directly towards his brother. The resulting fight was as intense as anything you would see on a Tom and Jerry cartoon. The two cats became a ball of tumbling fur and flailing legs but the worst thing of all was the noise. Katie could not believe that domestic animals, particularly her own babies, could sound so fierce. She threw herself towards them, with little regard for her own safety, but unfortunately tripped on a doorstop and fell head first into the mêlée. Her head hit the hall table, her hand hit the wall and the cats swiftly moved their fight upstairs. As Katie lay dazed the screaming stopped: Buttons had sought refuge under a chest of drawers in an impossibly narrow gap. Two broken fingers and a black eye later Katie still couldn't put the boys together without a rerun of this explosive encounter. Phil was devastated (and somewhat bemused) that his wife had incurred such dreadful injuries and insisted that one of the cats (at least) would have to go. At that point Katie remarked that Phil was more likely to go than either of the two cats if she had her way, but I wasn't sure this was necessarily the best option in the circumstances. I reassured her that it might not have to come to that and, without guaranteeing success, agreed to visit her to establish whether we could restore normality.

I arrived, as a matter of urgency, later that same week and sat opposite a very sorry-looking Katie to discuss the situation. Her right eye and cheek were swollen and two of her fingers were strapped up on her right hand. That really was some rugby tackle. Beau sat with us, showing great interest in my 'magic bag', and Buttons was sulking somewhere private upstairs. In the eight days since the accident Katie had become confident enough not to resort to shut doors during the day to separate the two cats. She did, however, keep them apart at night and the daytime was full of vigilance and preventative measures to avoid a repeat performance. There was, though, according to Katie, a great deal of posturing and swearing between the two. Beau was definitely the instigator of the aggression; Buttons hardly responded at all. Katie thought he looked rather bemused by the whole thing. He would occasionally chase Beau if he got fed up, apparently, but that was all.

I let Katie talk for a while (at last she had found someone

who truly understood) but soon steered her towards a more thorough history of their lives prior to the events of the previous week. She described a typical adult sibling relationship. The two boys did their own thing, occasionally resting in the same room together but mainly coexisting rather than enjoying each other's company. Probably an accident waiting to happen, but I did not hear anything particularly alarming until she started to talk about the last six months. She said that Buttons had become quite distressed by a series of decorating projects, both outside and inside the house. He had suffered from a couple of bouts of cystitis and inappropriate urination on the front doormat as a result, followed soon afterwards by a period of fur loss on his belly, described by the vet as 'probably stress-related'. Just as this problem seemed to be resolving he went down with an extremely high temperature and the laryngitis.

I put it to Katie that there was a possible link between the upheaval at home and the subsequent falling out between the brothers. The relationship had probably never been that brilliant once the siblings reached maturity. It simmered just like the one between Rhubarb and Hazel. Indoor cats have very predictable lives but any changes to their environment (their entire world, really) can potentially be quite distressing. I think Buttons took the brunt of this, so his stress levels increased, his immune system was compromised and his health suffered as a result. Stress works in layers, and the combination of changes, ill health and an annoying brother may have pushed him over the edge. He needed that water bowl on the landing and his brother muscling in to relieve his own sore throat was probably too much to bear. Beau then visits the vet, returns to see an approaching Buttons and decides a preemptive strike is probably advisable given the events of the previous day. The perfect recipe for a relationship breakdown.

As if on cue Buttons came downstairs and entered the room. Katie visibly stiffened and her voice became urgent and mildly frantic: 'What do I do, what do I do?' I asked her to focus on me and stop worrying, but as Beau hissed at Buttons, who continued to approach unperturbed, she said she couldn't cope and she had to intervene. She picked up Beau, who grumbled rather but continued to watch his brother. Buttons examined my bag, sniffed round generally, then went back into the hallway to use the litter tray. Beau remained under the table, breathing rapidly and nervously licking his lips. Buttons definitely had the upper paw here but the balance was so precarious I wasn't convinced it would stay that way.

I was keen to find out if either cat had injured the other during their fights. Katie replied that no physical harm appeared to have been done. In answer to several more of my questions, Katie was painting a picture of competition, passive aggression and guarding of strategic areas. The only difference pre- and post-apocalypse was that the aggression was more overt as their antagonism had reached a new level; it was finally all out in the open.

I was extremely pleased to see that the cats could at least be in the same room, but there was still a great deal of tension between them. More significantly, Katie was tense, and that had to stop. Owners understandably get very concerned when previously placid cats turn on each other. Unfortunately their anxiety adds to the feline tension, as I have said so many times before. It is easy to appreciate the significance of that in theory but another matter altogether for an owner to try to change and feel relaxed under these circumstances.

I gave Katie a programme to follow that increased the number of resources within the home to a level that should eliminate the need for Beau and Buttons to be so competitive. The often recommended 'one per cat, plus one, in different locations' is a good formula for all cat resources from litter trays to scratching posts and toys to water bowls. The house was rather short of private hiding places and high perches so we looked at various ways that Katie could enhance the ability of the the cats to get away from each other. Now came the important bit: how would Katie cope with changing herself? I bartered a little with her; after all, it's pointless asking someone to do something they honestly believe is beyond them, and we eventually agreed that she would try to relax, ignore the hissing and growling and (if really desperate to get involved) only employ distraction techniques such as moving across the room, talking to Phil or dragging a piece of string in front of the combatants. In no circumstances was she to scoop one up, reprimand the other or generally get involved in a complicated feline dispute. I also suggested, should the very worst happen, that she used my favourite technique of placing a cushion or pillow between the cats rather than a part of her body.

I awaited the first report with some trepidation but I really shouldn't have worried unduly. Katie was determined to make it work and, despite her husband's being pretty annoyed about the sudden abundance of litter trays, water bowls and scratching posts, she had approached her tasks with relish. She was *not* going to give up one of her boys no matter what it took to set things right again. Over the next few weeks she learnt to ignore the hissing by chanting a mantra in her head that went something like 'it's a cat thing, it's a cat thing'. I had tried to explain to her that a certain amount of aggressive posturing or noise was all part of everyday cat life and we really ought to let them say what needed to be said. It must have struck a chord because it was this thought that allowed her to relax sufficiently to see a significant improvement by the end of the two months. Beau and Buttons never really got back to normal (as far as I know) but Katie was happy enough and she realized she had been very fortunate to avoid the terrible decision to split them up.

❊   ❊   ❊

Whilst Hazel's and Beau's troubles started after a visit to the vet, it doesn't always happen that way. Redirected aggression can cause breakdowns too. Seeing a cat outside, fireworks, mail coming through the letterbox, a picture falling from the wall . . . there are so many sudden unexpected events that can make the adrenalin pump and cause your feline to release its pent-up emotions on the nearest available moving object. It is seldom something you can prevent, but following general guidelines about multi-cat living will limit the odds of your ever having to face it.

There are many potential problems associated with multi-cat living, the most common of which have been discussed in great detail in both *Cat Confidential* and *Cat Detective*. One such situation occurs when one member of the cat group dies. I have experienced this myself when three of my cats, Zulu, Puddy and Bln, tragically died within five months of each other. Cat groups usually have a deep respect for hierarchy and when one member is no longer there a shift in the balance of power almost always takes place. There usually one of three possible responses from the remaining cats, irrespective of how their 'rank' changes: they grieve, they blossom or they appear oblivious. This is often a good indication of the true relationship when the deceased cat was alive. Add the owner's emotions to this equation and things can get very complicated.

Tilly – the 'grieving' cat

Every now and then we meet a cat who rocks our world. Pookah was such a cat for his owners, Diane and Nick. I visited Diane only a few weeks after their beloved pet had passed away. Pookah had been diagnosed with cancer two years previously and he had valiantly coped with chemotherapy and operations during that period. He clearly had a wonderful personality; he was affectionate, demonstrative and larger than life. As Diane described her relationship with him it was apparent that she was finding it difficult to talk without breaking down and weeping. I saw photos and listened to her stories and began to feel that I really would have liked to meet this cat, such was her distress at his passing. The reason for my visit was a small ginger female, Tilly, who was hiding behind a table in the corner of the room. Tilly had been Pookah's constant companion throughout his life. Diane described the relationship between the two cats as 'one of tolerance rather than affection'. Tilly used to play a very secondary role, always in the background and never really part of the family. Pookah slept on the master bed and Tilly slept on the landing. Pookah sat on his owner's lap and Tilly sat on a cushion under the dining room table. Diane admitted that she was not a particularly rewarding cat to have around compared with Pookah.

When Pookah died both Diane and Nick were devastated. They had devoted such time and emotional energy to him and they missed him dreadfully. However, their grief was interrupted by Tilly's unexpected reaction. Suddenly she howled at night and paced and searched; she became a thing possessed. Diane was clearly affronted by this since she felt that Tilly, having shown no great affection for Pookah during his life, should not overindulge herself in demonstrative mourning rituals. I was shocked at the depth of her feelings about this; she even said at one point that she resented Tilly and wished it had been she who had passed away. Tilly continued to pace and howl until suddenly she committed the most heinous of crimes: she tried to take the place of Pookah in her owners' affections. Diane was furious, Tilly was confused and Vicky was asked to visit to make sense of it all. I tried, very gently, to explain to Diane what changes were taking place in Tilly's world.

Cat relationships are complex and often elements of personality expressed to human companions differ greatly from those shown to other cats. It was clear from the history that Pookah was more assertive than Tilly. He controlled access to his owners, the best seats in the house and the master bed. Tilly withdrew to a safe distance as a successful ploy to prevent bloodshed or, even worse, psychological warfare. She accepted defeat and was relatively content to live her life in the shadow of the dominant Pookah. When he died she was left with a real dilemma. Suddenly she was on her own. Where was he? What sinister strategy was he employing to further intimidate her? The distressed pacing and searching may well have been her attempt to restore the status quo; after all, better the devil you know. After a while, though, the scent profile of the home changes and surviving cats realize that their tormentors are no longer there. Tilly became more vocal, affectionate and inter-active because she now had access to her owners without incurring the wrath of her companion. She wasn't trying to take his place as such; she was merely enjoying her new-found freedom of expression. This phenomenon became apparent after I conducted research into the subject in the Elderly Cat Survey in 1995. Many people reported that cats blossomed after the death of a companion. Unfortunately it doesn't sit particularly comfortably with many owners, Diane and Nick included.

Diane was a caring and sensible lady and, when confronted with this new angle on the proceedings, she suddenly felt rather guilty. How could she have thought so ill of the little ginger cat? We talked about Pookah and grief and the loss of a beloved pet. We also discussed the possibility that Diane and Nick could develop a new relationship with Tilly without feeling guilty or imagining that it would in some way detract from the memory of dearest Pookah. I spoke to Diane the week after my visit and she reported a great improvement in her relationship with Tilly. The little ginger cat had relaxed enormously and now found that her approaches were received with love and kindness instead of hostility. I hope they are still enjoying each other's company.

Siobhan and her seven Singapore strays

I cannot resist including a story that illustrates so vividly the limitations of cat behaviour counselling! It may be an extreme example but it happened and it will probably make essential reading for those contemplating an exotic holiday in a place where feral cats are rife. I am not suggesting for one moment that we ignore their plight. We have all at some stage in our lives felt our heartstrings pulled by a skinny, scabby puss whilst on holiday. How many of us have returned to a certain spot time and again with food when we have seen a starving mite hanging around the back of the local hotels and restaurants? Occasionally the more determined cat lovers have gone just one step further and ended up paying high vet bills and even higher transport costs to take the little darling home. One such lady took this progression to another level.

Siobhan had lived for some years in Singapore with her husband. She was passionate about all things feline and she devoted her workless days to roaming the streets looking for waifs and strays. Or it certainly appeared so, as after five years she had acquired seven Singapore street cats of varying shapes and sizes, all of which were contained within the spacious surroundings of her air-conditioned apartment. They coexisted in relative harmony (or so she said when we met back in England some time later) but she actually described something quite different. It sounded to me as if the cats spent all day hiding in various dark areas until food was provided at night and the apartment was quiet. They didn't fight but I was suspicious that they had merely created a small feral colony in the confines of a beautiful airy apartment and dealt with the dissent in the group by shutting down. They urinated and defecated in several litter trays, if Siobhan was very lucky, or on the marble floor in various corners if she wasn't. I bet Siobhan's husband was thrilled.

The cats varied in their sociability with people but they all seemed to trust the lady who had 'saved' them from an uncertain fate. However, Siobhan had some reservations when it was decided that the couple would return to England. How would her babies cope with quarantine? Would they settle? Would they adjust to life outdoors or would they run away? By the time I met Siobhan she had been back in England for seven months and the cats were out of quarantine. Her husband had purchased a huge rambling Elizabethan pile in the middle of a wooded area in Sussex. It was full of exquisite period features and loads of nooks and crannies for seven Singapore street cats to get lost in. Surely they would be happy?

What I saw when I visited that house defied belief. Siobhan was so stressed and tense that she made me feel uptight within the first five minutes. She oscillated between tearful, hysterical and aggressive in a matter of seconds. I didn't know whether to pass her a tissue, sympathize or duck. The whole process was exhausting and not helped by the screams of various cats and a young Swedish girl who had been employed specifically to 'nanny' the warring felines and prevent bloodshed. The surreality was Monty Python-esque and I was completely per-plexed about what I was supposed to do with this tragic situation. I was feeling a bit of a challenge coming on.

I have seen many imported cats over the years, all of which have been 'saved' from a life on the streets. There is only one problem with this rescue strategy. These are cats used to living on their wits; they may become friendly and gooey with their new human companions but their response to other cats is often another matter. You may take the cat out of Singapore but you can't take Singapore out of the cat, you could say in this particular case. All seven of these cats were warring with the other six. Some were displaying active aggression and others were adopting various defence strategies to avoid being attacked. The ferocity of all of them was intense, as their world had become so terrifying they felt it was a case of kill or be killed. They were all surviving on red alert and I cannot even begin to contemplate how wretched they must have felt. Siobhan's histrionics were merely fuelling the fire, and the poor Swedish student must have felt that everyone in England was mad. They even employ cat behaviour counsellors!

There were at least three of the cats, particularly the eldest male, who needed to be rehoused. They found the concept of sharing impossible to grasp and made the situation extremely difficult for the whole group. 'Maybe if they were taken out of the equation it would be possible to work with the remaining four?' I tentatively suggested. Siobhan was adamant. They stayed together because she loved them and they loved her and no-one would look after them as well as she did. Well, that just about put the icing on this particular fruit cake so I gave her a programme to follow and bade her farewell. What a nightmare.

I received an abusive phone call the following morning. At least, that's what I thought it was initially until I realized the tirade of profanities was coming from Siobhan. One of the recommendations I had given her was to stop interfering so heavily in the cats' altercations except when they actually injured each other. She followed my advice, apparently, and one of the less confident cats had been attacked and chased out of a small window by the assertive male. She hadn't been seen since despite the Swedish nanny's doing several laps of the surrounding woodland with a bag of cat biscuits, a basket and a pair of stout gloves. This was clearly all my fault. In a strange way my heart went out to Siobhan that morning. She had acted with great compassion, albeit misplaced, when she 'rescued' her seven Singapore cats. She truly believed that she could provide them with a wonderful alternative to the misery of life as a feral. Had she stuck to one cat, probably the eldest male, the relationship might well have blossomed and she would have been rewarded for her generous act a thousandfold. Unfortunately poor Siobhan thought her cats were happy in her previous home and she would have been devastated to hear that their not fighting in the apartment was more a survival strategy than a sign of contentment. Rescuing no fewer than seven cats was seen by Siobhan as a symbol of her love for the species. When it all went horribly wrong back in England she was extremely distressed and she desperately needed to blame someone, anyone, for the disaster. I just happened to be in the firing line on that particular occasion.

The little cat was found some weeks later but there was no common ground between Siobhan and me. I gave her a programme to follow but it was eventually agreed that she would create two distinct units within her home, three cats to be housed on one side of the barrier and four on the other. It struck me as a ridiculous way to live when the alternative solution of splitting the group up would have been in the best interests of the cats. Unfortunately poor Siobhan couldn't see anything beyond keeping the cats together. We never spoke again but I hope the cats are OK and have reached some sort of compromise. If this story prevents even one group of cats from suffering a similar fate it has been well worth relating.

Gallons of urine and rubber sheets

I would like to end this chapter with a story about a case I never saw. It came to my attention during a book-signing event in a store in Devon whilst I was promoting my last book, *Cat Detective*. These evenings are always great fun: the store closes, the wine flows and cat lovers come from far and wide to enjoy a lively evening of feline facts and advice. We usually have a lengthy and often hilarious question and answer session during which we discuss everything from cat flaps to overgrooming and all subjects in between. The audience are almost always armed with reams of paper covered with questions and a good time is had by all. And there will always, always be a gem of a question. If you didn't know otherwise you could easily presume that these people are planted in the audience, such is the nature of their comments.

All was going well during the evening in Devon and there

was a great deal of laughter and banter and general high spirits. I had just finished a short session on keeping cats indoors and I was encouraging the audience to move on to another topic. In the middle of the room a gentleman had been sitting with his wife. I always like to check everyone out and I was pretty sure this chap had something on his mind. He had that slightly smug look on his face as if to say 'know that; know that too' so I was quite delighted when he raised his hand; I wanted to hear this one. I knew it was going to be a corker when he started with 'I've had cats for fifty-five years'. I nodded at him with an air of expectancy I could barely contain. He continued, 'I currently have thirty-five cats but have owned as many as forty in the past and they have always all got on well together.' Now I could have launched in there by challenging his statement most vehemently but it would have led nowhere. Let's just say I begged to differ with his appraisal of his cats' apparent happiness but I managed to contain myself with a wide-eyed expression and a quick 'Wow'. The audience were still buzzing as members continued various spin-off conversations but the room soon fell silent as our conversation progressed. He looked at his wife and she gave an encouraging nod as he said, 'The problem we have is that some of the cats are peeing on our bed at night.' Without showing any hint of I-told-you-so, I said, 'I see; how many of them are doing this?' He replied, 'We're not sure but we think it's about six of them.' I showed no emotion and no sign of surprise but the audience gasped. I continued, 'How often is this happening?' to which he replied, 'Every night.' Completely hooked, I casually asked, 'How long has this been going on?' He thought for a while, conferred with his wife, and then said, 'About four years.' You could have cut the atmosphere with a knife as I said quietly, 'Mmm, that's a lot of urine.'

I then acknowledged the audience's reaction by explaining to them that, unfortunately, it was the easiest thing in the world to find oneself in such a dreadful situation. Problems start and advice is followed, suggestions are made, litter trays are added and duvets are laundered. Suddenly, four years down the line, you are swimming in urine and your morning routine of washing duvets and wiping down rubber sheets comes as naturally as brushing your teeth. When he added that most of the urination on the bed took place when he and his wife were in it many of those present could not contain their disgust as an audible 'ergh' went round the room. The man asked if I would offer some advice or even consult in his home, but not before adding several priceless caveats: namely 'my cats aren't stressed; there's nothing wrong with their bladders; I'm not rehoming any and I think twelve litter trays are quite enough, thank you'.

I said 'Call me' and moved on to another question. He hasn't done so as yet but I have a horrible feeling that one day he will.

The secrets of a harmonious multi-cat household

- Start with two cats from the outset if you feel you want a multi-cat household; this is always easier than introducing 'No. 2' to 'No. 1'.
- Choose compatible individuals to share your home such as littermates, probably brother and sister. Two equal-age same-sex siblings may dispute the hierarchy when they mature socially.
- Avoid extreme characters when choosing kittens, for example extremely nervous, confident or active. These may potentially be difficult cats to live with or find others difficult to live with.

- If you want to adopt an adult cat, choose an individual that shows a history of sociability with other cats. Avoid those that have been given up for adoption because of behavioural problems in a previous multi-cat environment.
- There is no particular benefit in keeping kittens from your own cat's litter. Once the initial rearing process is complete the mother will naturally be ready to say goodbye.
- Keep an appropriate number of cats for your environment. This is particularly relevant if your cats are kept exclusively indoors.
- If there are many cats in the neighbourhood this fact will impact on your household too. Stick to two; if you have more cats in these circumstances it could increase the sense of overcrowding in your own group.
- Even if your cats have access to outdoors it is still advisable to provide indoor litter facilities. Then if there is any bullying going on outside your cats will always have the choice to toilet in comparative safety indoors.
- Avoid too many highly intelligent and sensitive pedigrees in the same household. Although most are the perfect pets, they can be extremely territorial or sensitive to inter-cat issues, particularly breeds such as Burmese, Bengal and Siamese.
- Remember your household will always have a 'one cat too many' threshold and you may push your luck if you keep increasing the numbers. If you have a harmonious foursome, for example, why not leave it that way!
- Social issues become important at the onset of maturity between eighteen months and four years of age. This is when you may experience problems between cats who have previously been friendly.
- Don't get too involved in your cats' disputes; it is impossible

to ensure you are reinforcing the right message. Some things need to be said between them but it doesn't always look nice.

- If you lavish constant attention on your cats you will yourself become a valuable resource. This can be dangerous and make your cats aggressive towards each other when you are around.

- Food, water, beds, hiding places, high perches, toys, scratching posts and litter trays should be provided in sufficient number to prevent competition. 'One per cat plus one in different locations' is the magic formula!

- Provide plenty of high resting places to enable any individuals to observe activity from a safe area.

- Private places are also extremely important; every cat, no matter how sociable, needs 'time out' to enjoy moments of solitude.

- Provide dry food for 'grazing' throughout the day or divide it into several smaller meals to avoid any sense of competition if food is only available at certain times. (Cats with a history of feline lower urinary tract disease or chronic cystitis should be fed a wet diet so ad lib dry food would not be appropriate.)

- Water is an important resource and positioning bowls away from food will encourage cats to visit them more frequently.

- Ensure there are plenty of scratching posts to protect your furniture. Cats will scratch for both claw maintenance and territorial reasons and there will be an increased need to signal to others in a multi-cat environment. These scratching posts should be located near entrances, exits, beds and feeding stations to ensure an appropriate surface is available in areas of potential competition.

- Studies have shown that the likelihood of urine spraying indoors increases in direct proportion to the number of cats in the household. You have been warned!

CHAPTER 3

Where Do You Go To, My Lovely?

IF YOUR CAT HAS ACCESS TO THE GREAT OUTDOORS THEN YOU know there is a huge chunk of his activity about which you know very little. How many people can honestly say they know exactly what their cat is doing once he exits the cat flap in the morning? Wouldn't it be great if all our cats could be fitted with tiny cameras so that we could get a true understanding of their feline 'day at the office'?

There are some things we do know, through research on feral colonies and house-cat territories conducted by biologists such as Roger Tabor. This shows us that a cat's world is divided into three recognized areas:

- the 'core' area or den

- the territory
- the home range

The core area

This is the area within which your cat feels most secure. This is where he sleeps deeply, plays, eats and enjoys all the benefits of cohabiting with humans. It is such a safe place to be that any prey he catches during his hunting forays will often be brought back there so he can enjoy it without being disturbed. As we represent such an element of security, the core area is almost automatically the home itself; however, if there is an established opening or cat flap into the property this may create a rather blurred picture of what represents the safe den. The core area may then be, for example, the first floor (it's always safer to go 'up' in your cat's mind) or it may be the room where the family congregates most frequently. Disputes in multi-cat households may also affect the perception of the core area for less confident individuals.

The territory

Whilst the core area forms the hub of the territory there is a whole other world that is included for the cat with access outside. The territory is defined as that area the cat actively defends against invasion by others. The size of this area will vary greatly with each individual and depend on season, level of confidence, sex, density of population and many other factors. Your cat may take Sooty's face off if he dares to venture onto the patio but not flick a whisker if he sees him further down the garden. Cats don't respect their owners' boundaries as a representation of defendable property; they are not governed by fences, hedges and walls. Territories often include roads, waste land, other people's gardens and anything in between.

Home range

This includes the territory but describes the total area over which your cat will roam. I have seen many 'feline friendly' streets where some poor cats are lucky to call the bottom of the garden their own. In Roger Tabor's 1976–78 study in East London he found that those females included had a home range of the garden plus any further space that their confidence and the density of population would allow. A typical home range in a densely populated area is 0.05 acres for a neutered female, although neutered males often roam further.

❄   ❄   ❄

Your cat will spend his day patrolling; scent marking using his face, body and paws and generally checking to see who's about. The type of encounter with other cats outside will vary depending on how territorial your cat is, how territorial the other cat is and where the eyeballing takes place. Many cats can be seen sitting within a respectful distance of each other in apparent harmony and yet the same two cats will be fighting tooth and claw the next day in another location. Your cat will also be spending time hunting (if so inclined), sunning himself, sleeping in secret dense bushes and hopefully staying out of trouble. Sadly some don't and they spend time breaking into other people's houses and terrorizing their cats, getting shut in garden sheds, fighting, killing birds or playing chicken with the traffic. It's not hard to understand why so many cat lovers want to keep their pets at home where they can see them.

I won't be dwelling on the theoretical stuff of the great outdoors in this chapter because I want to focus on the sorts of problems that arise as a result of giving your cat his freedom. I certainly don't want to put anyone off making the decision to let their cat outside. This is by far the most natural lifestyle and cats who can behave normally are more likely to be mentally healthy. However, there are a lot of other cats, people and cars out there, and some issues and quandaries are common to many owners.

Returning to a previous home

One subject I get many calls on throughout each year is the problem of cats returning to previous homes. This can be extremely distressing since they often have to cross busy roads to get there. There seem to be some common elements to most of the cases, such as:

- the cat had previously spent a great deal of time outside
- the cat was considered to be territorial on his 'patch'
- the cat lived with at least one other, often a sibling
- the house move was within a mile of the previous home

This is a difficult situation as the cat in question is voting with his paws. It is entirely likely that his bond was with the environment and not the family and that the house move was confusing and highly undesirable. The cat might well have spent so much time outdoors as a result of a poor relationship with his or her sibling, and the prospect of being confined in a strange place with someone it dislikes is too much to bear. Navigation in these circumstances is astonishing but highly achievable for cats. Owners of such wanderers report that after several days they will receive a phone call from an ex-neighbour saying that the cat is hanging round the garden of the old house, crying pitifully. In my experience these cats rarely come 'home' to their new abode on their own; the owner collects them only to face exactly the same thing when the cat is next let outside. I am often asked if the cat should be confined indoors for prolonged periods to get acclimatized to the new house. This is a dangerous strategy since it may only fuel his desire to escape at the next possible opportunity.

Unfortunately there is no easy solution to this problem. A product called 'Feliway' (synthetic feline pheromones) is available from your vet practice and a useful addition to the new property. It can be purchased in a plug-in form and the scent message that it emits may give your cat a better perception of the new house as home. Small frequent tasty meals can sometimes be helpful, together with plenty of opportunities indoors to get away from other cats. Persistence in retrieving the wanderer from your old house is the key, with the aid of a co-operative ex-neighbour, together with strict instructions to everyone not to feed him. If the relationship between your cats is really not good (and the new occupiers of the old property are amenable) it may be in his best interests to let him stay there.

The wanderer exposed

Some wandering cats are not necessarily returning to previous homes and favoured stomping grounds. Consider the opportunistic cat who cannot resist the chance of commandeering as many homes as possible within a given area. A cat with four owners travels between each one depending on his own personal whims; each owner believes they are having an exclusive monogamous relationship with their cat and he just goes off 'hunting' from time to time. This cat may well be seriously over-vaccinated and even registered twice with the same vet in one village (under different names, of course). I have received hundreds of letters over the years detailing problems but many owners just want to tell me their stories; fascinating. One letter I read back in the early nineties is particularly relevant.

We acquired Marmalade with this house, which we purchased two years ago. The previous owners had taken him on in the same way, as had the owners before him. Marmalade is well known (notorious) in the neighbourhood. He has obviously, in the past, roamed over most of this valley. He is known to be eighteen years old, and is thought to be considerably older. He has only one ear and his back legs are skinny and bent with age. His tongue is usually hanging out because the few teeth he still has are at the back of his mouth. He doesn't seem to be able to miaow any more, but can and does purr very loudly. His old owners told us that he often went missing for several days at a time, and then reappeared; they put this down to hunting trips. Sure enough, this pattern continued for several months after we moved in. Then the girl next door came to tell us she was moving out and would we please look after her little ginger cat, which was very old and went hunting for days at a time!

This is just another illustration of our complete gullibility when faced with a loving cat in apparent need of a good home; we never really *own* cats at all, do we?

The next few cases illustrate the complexity of the concept of territory. It is safe to say that situations of this kind could happen to any one of us.

Billy Bob – the reluctant defender

Billy Bob and Joey were two Orientals who had a great relationship. They adored each other and they adored their owner, Jackie, and this triangular love-fest continued for twelve glorious years. Jackie became the sort of owner who believed that cats loved other cats and feline company was everything because they enjoyed the experience. Billy Bob used to follow Joey and go on great adventures with him through the adjoining gardens. They had a cat flap and they came and went as they pleased. It was a perfectly balanced and enjoyable existence for all until Joey became ill. He was diagnosed with a tumour and over a period of four weeks he deteriorated until the time came for him to be peacefully put to sleep at home. Jackie chose this option to ensure that Billy Bob understood that Joey had died and wouldn't be coming back. She was quite surprised by Billy Bob's reaction on the day; he seemed relatively unmoved. After Joey's body was taken away, however, he began to display his grief. He paced, he wailed like a banshee, he searched and, when he wasn't doing all that, he clung to his owner. His distress was palpable. He stopped eating and poor Jackie didn't know what to do to ease his suffering. Worse was to come when Billy Bob jumped up on Jackie's bed one morning and urinated all over her pillow. This isn't a wake-up call that any cat owner relishes but she cleaned up after him and forgave him his indiscretion. After all, he was in mourning and he had been behaving out of character since

Joey's death. Unfortunately it wasn't a one-off and several incidents later Jackie contacted me for my help and guidance at a very difficult time.

When I met Billy Bob I was overwhelmed by his tension and distress, and his behaviour towards Jackie was extraordinary. He watched her all the time, he touched her whenever he could and every time she sat down he jumped all over her. If he could have unzipped her skin and climbed inside he would have done. I asked Jackie whether this was normal for him and she reported that his clingy behaviour had only started since Joey's demise. Prior to that the two cats had appeared relatively self-reliant, merely spending evenings curled up on her lap whilst she watched television. She had never previously found it difficult to move around the flat because of a cat at her feet. She had certainly never found it hard to leave her house either, unlike now, when every excursion had to be carefully planned to take the minimum amount of time. Every time she returned she dreaded the sight of a urine-stained duvet or pillow.

In order to understand this apparent change in personality it was necessary to look again at the relationship between Billy Bob and Joey. The apparent affection between the two cats was actually something rather more dysfunctional. What had appeared to be a sociability born of a desire to spend time with each other was actually a dependency. Their relationship was based on need not want and Billy Bob was suffering from the symptoms of withdrawal from his addiction to Joey.

Over many years breeders have attempted to create the ultimate sociable cat. Many breeds are described by their 'dog-like' behaviour. I suppose the fact is that we want pets for emotional reasons and we expect a relationship to develop that gives back what we put in. Dogs are ideal for this purpose but many of us work and cannot devote the necessary time and energy to their care. So we develop a cat that behaves like a dog and, hey presto, we have the perfect compromise. Or do we? I often wonder whether trying to improve on nature is truly in the best interests of the species we profess to love so much. Are we really creating a sociable pack animal in the body of a territorial solitary predator with absolutely no adverse consequences, or are we actually achieving something else entirely?

I explained to Jackie that I had felt for some time that many apparently sociable cats, either with people or with each other, were merely exhibiting a dependency. Susceptible individuals find self-reliance too difficult to achieve and they learn very quickly that clinging to another provides the security they crave. Whilst this is great all the time the two parties are together it poses a dreadful dilemma when one isn't there any more. Billy Bob had reached this point and transferred his dependency to Jackie. The only problem with this arose when it came to defending the territory against invading cats. This had always been Joey's job and he had patrolled the area fearlessly (with Billy Bob several paces behind), keeping all potential adversaries at bay. The word had soon got out that Joey was no more and the more daring and opportunistic members of the local community had started to investigate what exactly it was that Joey had been defending so vehemently. What they found was Billy Bob, a nice bit of garden, a cat flap and loads of food. His garden was no longer the safe fortress it used to be and toileting in the flower bed became fraught with danger. Billy Bob just wasn't equipped to do Joey's job and he wallowed in a mire of insecurities and phobias. No amount of vocalizing to his owner was getting the point across that danger was present; I'm positive that Billy Bob thought Jackie pretty useless when it came to defence of their castle. When he needed to urinate desperately he found the soft yielding surface of his owner's bed and the strong positive scent message too much to resist, so voided his bladder in this safe location. Given his character and circumstances I would defy anyone to do otherwise. I felt an equal amount of sympathy for both Billy Bob and Jackie; this was a difficult situation.

It is impossible to get into the head of the scared and in-secure cat and tell him to 'pull yourself together'. I wish it was that simple. Billy Bob had lost the plot and everything frightened him. He had turned to Jackie for support and guidance at a time when she was least able or willing to give it. Not only was she grieving for Joey, but Billy Bob was peeing on her bed! I had to devise a plan that would return the relationship to one with a more manageable level of interaction and, somehow, restore a little confidence in Billy Bob so that he could at least function relatively independently. It was an extremely difficult problem to address because there were so many complications and practical considerations. If we blocked up the cat flap and stopped the invading forces from entering and terrorizing Billy Bob we would merely push him further into the arms of his owner. He would become totally reliant on her to give him entry and exit to the home. This would reinforce his insecurities tenfold and make him even less able to function as a fully fledged cat. If, however, we didn't shut the cat flap his adversaries would continue to gain entry and he would undoubtedly continue to pee on Jackie's duvet.

The added complication I have not mentioned until now was Billy Bob's complete aversion to all things resembling litter trays. This made it impossible for us to confine him indoors for any period of time without risking an assault on the pillow. We did try to give him every type of tray and litter known to man (even soft incontinence pads) but he wasn't fooled by any of it and retained urine to bursting point rather than pee anywhere but his owner's bed.

Lateral thinking, as always, saved the day in this particular case. Both Jackie and I were at our wits' end and rehoming had been mentioned several times. Part of me felt this was an option worth considering but I knew that Jackie, deep down, would do anything to get things back to how they used to be when Joey was alive. I came up with a plan. Billy Bob wasn't going anywhere very much these days. He would patrol outside somewhat reluctantly but avoided any temptation to go beyond the relatively predictable space of his own back yard. The surrounding fencing was high and the whole area lent itself to the concept of a 'secure garden'. We therefore agreed that any holes in the fence would be repaired and a series of inverted pillars and netting would be attached to the top of the fence to make the space safe from future invasions.

The process was watched with great interest by Billy Bob and it was soon time for him to explore his fortified domain. I asked Jackie to wash the patio and soak the plants and turn over the soil to provide a 'blank canvas' of scent for Billy Bob to explore. Within the first day Jackie was delighted to report that she had observed Billy Bob urinating under the pyracantha. What a result!

Poppy and the girls – the curse of the cat flap

Anyone who has read my previous books will know I am not a big fan of the cat flap. I do, however, understand that they are a necessary evil since many cats would be deprived of the opportunity to go outside if they didn't have one. None the less

I cannot resist offering a cautionary tale just in case your cat flap has become more of a curse than a blessing.

Rachel and her boyfriend lived with four female moggies, Poppy, Smudge, Angel and a rather petite cat called Belle. The first three were all around the same age, ten or eleven, and Belle was the baby at the tender age of three. They lived in a pleasant cul-de-sac of semi-detached houses in Surrey and they hadn't had a care in the world with their feline family until a couple of months before Rachel called me. All four cats seemed to get on really well; they came and went and had complete freedom. So why, suddenly, had Belle started spraying urine in the house and Smudge peeing on the carpet? This was a terrible shock for Rachel and she was desperately trying to understand what was happening. She felt either it was something she was doing or her cats had inexplicably decided to become dirty.

I visited Rachel to put her mind at rest about the whole 'dirty protest' thing and to get to the bottom of the recent dramatic changes in behaviour. Poppy, Smudge, Angel and Belle did indeed have complete freedom to come and go via a cat flap in the wall of the spacious lounge/diner leading to the back garden. When I sat talking to Rachel I was surrounded by a 'posse comitatus' of felines, arranged strategically in various positions in the room. Belle was crouched by the cat flap, Poppy was on the table in the dining area, Smudge was on the arm of a chair and Angel was on the window sill. They were trying to look relaxed and casual about the whole thing but I had a sense that they were coiled springs waiting to act at the first sign of trouble. The fact that they were all facing towards the cat flap didn't go unnoticed either.

As I suspected, there had been a new neighbour's cat coming in through the flap and stealing their food recently. Rachel, like so many owners, felt this wasn't such a big issue since all four cats had witnessed the invasions at one time or another and only one, the diminutive Belle, had offered any challenge. Rachel was more concerned about the behaviour between the 'four girls' as she called them. A tension had arisen among them and she was positive that the innocent-looking Belle was behind it all. She had taken to sitting in front of the cat flap and guarding it. As Belle's unsuspecting victim entered the perceived safety of the home she was bopped heavily by a small but powerful paw. The recipient of the blow would then scream and either reverse out again or vanish to the sanctuary of a wardrobe to ponder on the whole unpleasantness. Poppy, Smudge and Angel were, however, taking some revenge for this display of thuggery, according to Rachel. All four cats had previously slept on their owners' bed at night (I often wonder if the increasing sale of oversized beds is anything to do with this sort of sleeping arrangement?) but recently the older three had found one companion conspicuous by her absence. Belle had taken to sleeping in the living room alone. Was this a defensive measure or something Belle had decided of her own free will? There had also been a number of scraps between the four cats; Angel had taken to disappearing off to a quiet corner, poor Smudge had started voting with her bottom and urinating in the corner of the bedroom and Belle had been seen several times spraying urine in various locations in the living room and kitchen. Poppy seemed rather ill at ease too and something was clearly not right.

Whilst I could clearly see the animosity I wasn't convinced that the girls' deteriorating relationship was the primary cause of the problem. My finger of suspicion pointed firmly towards the invading cat from No. 6. After all, how could aggravated burglary three times a week *not* be an issue? During the consultation I experienced something that all cat owners should look out for, especially those who haven't considered the potential implications of the cat flap. Smudge and Angel were still occupying sunny spots in the living room but Belle had wandered into the kitchen and Poppy had returned to the warmth of the fleece by the radiator in the bedroom. Suddenly the cat flap rattled with a gust of wind and Smudge and Angel launched themselves high into the air. They landed simultaneously and crouched in readiness for the ensuing invasion. Nothing came, but they continued to be vigilant. I tried to explain to Rachel that the cat flap was no longer the convenient 'open all hours' access to the great outdoors; it was now the portal of Hades to her feline companions.

Belle was spraying urine due to a changed perception of the boundaries of her safe haven. The ground floor had become a no man's land where rights of ownership were being constantly challenged. It represented nothing better than the garden or surrounding properties and was therefore worthy of as much marking activity as the bushes and fences outside. She felt compelled to guard the flap as often as possible (somebody had to) and her constant desire to go in and out was everything to do with patrolling and checking and nothing to do with a pleasant constitutional. Smudge was just too terrified to pee outside with the threat of the beast from No. 6 ever present so she retained urine to bursting point then flooded the shag pile when she could hold no longer. Tensions were high and all four cats started to take it out on each other in desperate acts of redirected aggression.

The solution to this sort of problem is to redefine the boundaries of the house as a zone of safety. Cat flaps don't signal security to cats (it's a little like leaving the front door open when you go away on holiday) so they rarely form part of a therapy programme to restore a sense of safety. Unfortunately the provision of exclusive-entry cat flaps, together with magnetic keys on collars, once a house has been invaded, is rarely enough. It may prevent all but the most determined interloper from gaining access but the concept is a little complicated for the average cat to grasp. Any invasion changes everything and no amount of magnetism will make an ounce of difference.

We had to take more drastic measures to restore harmony and this in itself created other potential problems. If we blocked the cat flap completely, so that it disappeared from view, it left the resident cats in one of two distinct places at any one time: either outside or inside. Few owners would feel happy about suddenly leaving their cats out all day or night, and probably rightly so in this busy world. Entry and exit would only be achieved with the help of either Rachel or her boyfriend and they weren't always at home to be at the beck and call of their charges. The other potential risk is that the enemy is actually within the house when the flap is shut and battle commences as stress levels reach fever pitch. I discussed the options at some length with Rachel but she was extremely concerned that the cats would be largely confined to the house apart from times when she was there. We eventually agreed on a compromise and installed the formulaic number of litter trays indoors to satisfy Smudge and ensure the carpet was no longer seen as the only suitable latrine. Rachel agreed to shut the cat flap at night and keep the cats in to gauge their response to this new regime.

She reported later that week that the first night was fraught with anxiety. All six of them were huddled together listening to the relentless banging of the cat flap as the cat from No. 6 tried as hard as he could to break in. Belle didn't even venture downstairs, such was the ferocity of his endeavours. Squirts of sprayed urine were everywhere in the living room and kitchen when Rachel returned from work the following evening. Things were not going well, but at least Smudge et al thought the new litter facilities were a great idea. Rachel was also greeted that evening by almost everything the four cats could produce, in the urine and faeces department, neatly piled up in the new toilets. The trays were clearly a success for them but this just represented another chore for Rachel, unfortunately. After the first week she was exhausted and she agreed that we had to renegotiate the whole cat flap thing. She and her boyfriend started to plan their diaries and, after careful consideration of shift patterns and flexitime, it was discovered that their working life could be adjusted to such an extent that the house would only be empty for a couple of hours during the day. This was a breakthrough and steps were taken to board up the cat flap at the front and back of the opening. Soon the wall appeared solid again.

For the next few weeks Rachel and her boyfriend were constantly on the go, letting them all in or out on demand. Nevertheless, there was an increased friction between the cats and a significant rise in active fighting. I was concerned that my worst fear had been realized and the enemy was indeed within the home. Luckily, dutifully reported by Rachel, it was a temporary setback and the cats soon adjusted to their new regime. The cat from No. 6 must have been confused to be faced with a blank wall where a flap and a free meal once stood but he probably got the message and sightings became sporadic. The best news of all was that Belle stopped spraying urine on the pedal bin and the CD rack. The toaster, settee and curtains were untouched and the house stopped smelling of urine and fear.

A few months later Rachel experimented and took the dangerous step of re-establishing the cat flap, at least during the day, so that she could return to her previous working hours. She had discussed this with her boyfriend and they felt the cat from No. 6 had been absent for long enough to give it a go. Six months later she phoned me to report that all was back to normal. The girls were relaxed with each other but happy to remain indoors with the cat flap locked during the night. The litter trays, after the initial novelty had worn off, were being used by Smudge and Angel only, so Rachel had removed two of them to reduce the extra work and expense of servicing so many. Belle had not sprayed for seven and a half months and (touch wood) Rachel felt we had cracked it. I agreed, at least until the next time . . .

Tinker – or Genghis Khan to his friends

If you have read *Cat Confidential* you may remember the case of Hercules, the despotic Burmese. Rarely are cases more frustrating than those that involve third parties and their pets. I cannot complete a chapter on the cat's relationship with its territory and all within it without focusing once again on this unfortunate phenomenon. All cats should be territorial, it is an important survival strategy for a solitary predator, but many domestic cats maintain a measured response when exercising this natural behaviour. They may scrap in their garden if Sooty comes a-calling with evil on his mind but they don't go looking for trouble. Sadly, some cats take the concept of 'natural behaviour' to another level.

Tinker was a beautiful two-year-old snow-leopard-spotted Bengal. He was a masterpiece of creative perfection, all muscle and silky fur, and I could certainly see his appeal. His owners Anita and Simon were captivated by his charm and good looks and he appeared to be the perfect pet. I, of course, knew otherwise; the mere fact that I was there was a bad sign.

Tinker and his owners lived in a residential area in Berkshire. They had a big house and garden surrounded by other large properties and the bottom of the garden backed on to a quiet cul-de-sac of bungalows. It was an obvious haven for cats and, for the first two years of his life, Tinker seemed to enjoy the delights of the outdoors and the comforts of the home in equal measures. He was a perfect, loving pet – prone, in my opinion, to extreme manipulation of Anita, who was absolute putty in his paws, but nothing that would constitute a treatable problem. Most owners would have relished his affectionate, gentle and slightly naughty character. And then, one day, Anita and Simon received the shock of their lives. They discovered that, for some time, Tinker had been leading a double life. Simon had a phone call from an elderly gentleman called John. He lived in one of the bungalows in the cul-de-sac behind their house and he had indulged in quite a bit of detective work to find out their identity, address and telephone number. He had been looking for the owners of 'Genghis Khan'.

Apparently (and this was astounding to Simon) Tinker had quite a reputation locally; hence the pseudonym. John and several of his neighbours had known of his presence for some time. He was, after all, a handsome and distinctive beast, but his looks were no compensation for his recent heinous acts of violence. Simon listened as John related tales of victimization, break-ins and vicious attacks, but he wasn't prepared for the next revelations. John's cat Fluffy had been a regular recipient of a good bashing from 'Genghis'. If this wasn't bad enough, the attacks had all taken place in the supposed safety of Fluffy's home. Tinker had burst through the cat flap and actively sought out his victim, minding his own business on the kitchen chair. John had only seen the retreating tail disappearing through the cat flap when he had rushed to his pet's rescue before, but last night was different. John managed to get himself between Tinker and the cat flap and he made a grab for him to push him away from defenceless Fluffy. Tinker turned and lunged at John with teeth and claws and the poor man ended up in Casualty. All Simon wanted to say in response to this was 'You are obviously mistaken; this cannot be our Tinkiepoos' but somehow, deep down, he knew John was telling him the truth. Tinker had obviously been playing around with chemicals and potions and managed to effect a Jekyll and Hyde-type transformation. There could be no other explanation.

Simon, all credit to him, confronted the serious nature of this information immediately. Within forty-eight hours I was sitting in his kitchen, with both owners and a wide-eyed, purring Tinkiepoos. He had been confined to barracks since the call from John to show the couple's determination to stop this nightmare. They were, I think, hoping that I could confirm their suspicions of Tinker's long hours in the laboratory (figuratively speaking) and produce an antidote that would return him to normal. I had to take a deep breath and explain that this wasn't something that could be fixed; this was the nature of the beast. Some years ago stories of this kind almost always included a handsome Burmese. Now that the popularity of the Bengal has reached incredible levels I now feel that they have become the new Burmese (only, with spots or stripes). The situation has to be seen in the right perspective, though; there are a lot of Burmese and Bengals out there and most of them make perfect pets. However, when they go wrong . . .

Anita and Simon had exactly the same dilemma as Ted and Angela had with Hercules. John was being perfectly co-operative but was adamant about his inability to confine his cat. My suggestions, given to Simon prior to my visit, of time-share arrangements and cat-flap blocking at night were non-starters when he broached the subject with John. We explored cat-proofing the garden; we even went down the dubious route of investigating wireless fencing systems that involved giving Tinker low current electric shocks when he approached Fluffy's cat flap, but we had become quite desperate by then. Tinker could not be confined so Anita and Simon started ringing John when Tinker was outside to pre-pare him for attack. John would ring back as soon as Tinker entered his garden, and Anita or Simon would rush round and collect their cat before too much damage was done. This was working in a fashion but all life had stopped to accommodate Tinker's violent streak and the strain was showing.

The following weekend I remember several tearful phone calls with Anita. Tinker had just started to spray urine indoors (and allegedly in several other neighbours' homes) and this really made Anita think that she was keeping a cat in circum-stances that were making him deeply unhappy. Was she being selfish? The biggest dilemma when dealing with these cats is twofold: convincing the owners that rehoming is a feasible option and finding a home on a relatively small island that will accommodate a cat with such grand-scale ideas of territory. Anita and Simon were absolutely brilliant and the selfless and painful decision they made that weekend still makes me emotional. Unlike Hercules' owners they didn't have a conveniently placed aunt in the middle of the Outer Hebrides or a friend of a friend on the Yorkshire Moors. Their friends and family were no better placed to give Tinker a home than

Simon and Anita themselves. The calls and emails from them were gut-wrenching: 'Can't we just drug him? Do we have to give him up?' When they eventually decided to take him to a rural cat rescue centre (with prior agreement, given his special circumstances) they drove back twice with the sole purpose of bringing him away again. I can only imagine how heart-breaking that must have been and I will always admire their courage.

So, Tinker found himself in an adoption centre with a prominently displayed notice on his cage reading:

Tinker is a highly territorial cat, very much as nature intended for the feline. This is an inherent characteristic and, if presented with a number of cats in close proximity within his territory, he will be proactive in his aggression. He will not tolerate cohabiting with another cat so he needs to find a home as a singleton. It would probably be advisable for the home not *to have a cat flap.*

Despite his aristocratic good looks he has the needs of a hunting/shooting/fishing feral and a wide open space would be ideal, with plenty of opportunities to forage, explore and hunt. A small-holding or rural environment would be perfect. He will continue to fight if presented with other cats in his home range but this is the nature of the beast. He will, paradoxically, be a wonderful affectionate kitten-cat for his new owners. Tinker is the true 'tiger in your living room'.

The law and your cat

Over the past couple of years I have seen a worrying trend emerge in the type of phone calls I am receiving. There has been an alarming rise in the cases involving disputes between neighbours resulting from disputes between their cats. Tinker's case is a typical example of the despotic cat causing havoc; other cases include injuries to neighbours, damage to property and compensation demanded for vet bills. I am extremely reluctant to get involved in these cases so I hope the next few paragraphs will be helpful to all those poor souls who find themselves in this predicament.

A couple of years ago there was a rather disturbing article in the London *Evening Standard* newspaper about a five-year-old Bengal. The sensational piece of journalism accused him of fighting with every cat in his neighbourhood, killing one and leaving two others so severely traumatized that they had to be put to sleep. The rest of the story had familiar themes that I had experienced many times before. The owners were in complete denial; they insisted that their beloved pet was not vicious but they had agreed to erect an outdoor pen for him and confine him during the day. The neighbours had formed an action group and the police had become involved. The owners of the injured parties insisted on compensation for their extensive vet bills and the language was emotive and confrontational. The Bengal's attack cry was described as 'bloodcurdling' and his walk was 'like a leopard on the prowl'. There was even a reference to Bengals' being classified as wild cats rather than domestic pets. Death threats had been made by desperate neighbours; one had allegedly said that he would despatch the Bengal once and for all with the aid of a heavy garden implement.

I was severely traumatized myself by this story, although I have never yet been involved in a case of territorial aggression where a cat was killed or put to sleep as a result of its injuries. As far as I could tell from the article none of the attacks were witnessed and the injuries sustained could well have resulted from other causes. However, the frightening fact is that any cat, especially a large muscular cat like a Bengal, is perfectly capable of killing another cat. The reason why this doesn't happen more often is a result of generations of domestication and a diluting of the territorial instinct that allows cats to cohabit without ripping each other apart. Most cats will defend their territory, either passively through threat and intimidation or actively through violence. I have to admit that Bengals and Burmese are over-represented in cases of extreme territorial aggression, but maybe this is just a trait that has been bred into them by accident?

I have been concerned for some time now that very soon such cases will go to court. It has always been understood that cats are classified in law as 'free spirits', beyond the control of the owner as they roam by nature. However, we cannot get away from the fact that they do cause damage and they do fight, resulting in high veterinary bills. Even given the pro-tection of the term 'free spirit' there seems to be increasing pressure to review cats' culpability. One day very soon a frustrated owner will seek damages from the owner of a warring cat; I'm not sure I would like to be an expert witness but I'll have to be in the public gallery for that one.

I'm no lawyer but I wonder how relevant the Animals Act 1971 would be when discussing liability for damage or injury caused by a pet cat if the 'free spirit' angle became invalid as an excuse?

The Animals Act 1971

Extracts from Section 2

2 Where damage is caused by an animal which does not belong to a dangerous species, a keeper of the animal is

liable for the damage, except as otherwise provided by this Act, if:

- the damage is of a kind which the animal, unless restrained, was likely to cause or which, if caused by the animal, was likely to be severe; and
- the likelihood of the damage or of its being severe was due to characteristics of the animal which are not normally found in animals of the same species or are not normally so found except at particular times or in particular circumstances; and
- those characteristics were known to that keeper or were at any time known to a person who at that time had charge of the animal who is a member of that household and under the age of sixteen.

Extracts from Section 5

1   A person is not liable under sections 2 to 4 of this Act for any damage which is due wholly to the fault of the person suffering it.

2   A person is not liable under section 2 of this Act for any damage suffered by a person who has voluntarily accepted the risk thereof.

3   A person is not liable under section 2 of this Act for any damage caused by an animal kept on any premises or structure to a person trespassing there, if it is proved either: that the animal was not kept there for the protection of persons or property; or (if the animal was kept there for the protection of persons or property) that keeping it there for that purpose was not unreasonable.

I've read the Animals Act several times and it raises some important questions for cat owners. Could a cat owner be held liable for his or her pet's behaviour? The query I have concerning Section 2 relates to the interpretation of 'normal' behaviour for the species and prior knowledge of 'characteristics'. There will always be a debate about what is normal or abnormal; you could argue that it is abnormal for a cat *not* to fight with another in its territory. In fact a great deal of what the domestic cat gets up to these days arguably isn't normal for the species. If you knew that your cat, like the Bengal in the newspaper article, was particularly aggressive and that it was almost inevitable he would get in a fight every day and cause injury, would this make you liable for the damage he caused? There is no need to be proved negligent to be liable under the Act. However, if I have interpreted Section 5 correctly, you wouldn't be liable if the damage was the fault of the person suffering it, or if they had voluntarily accepted the risk of its happening to them. Could you describe it as 'fault' if an owner intervened between two fighting cats and got injured as a result? Do you 'voluntarily accept' the risk of injury or damage to your property if you fit a cat flap?

I apologize for ending this chapter with questions and no answers. As far as I am aware there is currently no legal precedent for cases of this kind. I may be worrying completely unnecessarily, but the volume of calls I receive on this very subject is increasing daily. My own opinion is that we should all accept that cats are solitary predators, defenders of territory and potentially dangerous creatures. That is the nature of the beast. We have a moral duty, as good citizens, to listen to neighbours' grievances and take reasonable measures to address their complaints if the alleged 'attacks' take place in their own home. However, we also have a duty to our own cats to take every precaution to ensure that our homes are suitably protected from invasion by other cats. Therefore I honestly believe it is the victim's responsibility to maintain the security of the property. Cats will fight; it is a natural behaviour and some cats are more natural than others. There have to be occasions in life when the compensation culture does not apply.

CHAPTER 4

Cats and All Things Furred, Feathered and Finned

FISH, HAMSTERS, GERBILS, MICE, BIRDS AND RATS, TO NAME but a few, are all common household pets. Many families also have cats, but this combination is naturally the pairing of a hunter and its prey. There are countless anecdotal stories about unusual relationships arising between such mismatched species but caution is the key word; you really don't want Sooty running off with your child's hamster in a moment of madness. Many cats, however, if brought up with other species, will develop friendships that defy nature. They will see all living things around them as part of the social group and behave accordingly.

I have a very good friend, Pete, who was persuaded by a local zoo to take on a meerkat. This particular individual had been hand-reared after being rejected by his mother and proved impossible to integrate back into the group. The meerkat is a social creature and the zookeepers felt that my friend's menagerie (including eight cats, two dogs, many ferrets and even more gerbils) would be sufficient company for any such gregarious beastie. To cut a long and fraught story short, the young meerkat settled in extremely well and I have several photographs of him with any one of the eight cats, holding their faces in a vice-like grip with his front paws and washing them like there was no tomorrow. He also has a habit of sitting on their backs and rummaging through their fur for fleas. The cats accept both activities with good grace and a look of great contentment. These cats had become accustomed to sharing their home with dogs, ferrets, tortoises, seagulls, lambs and any other waifs and strays that needed Pete's attention; another species made little difference to them. They merely embraced the meerkat behaviours that pleased them and left the little fellow in no doubt about those that didn't. It never ceases to amaze me that cats can turn any situation to their advantage.

Probably the most popular companion for our favourite pet is a canine friend. There is occasionally what appears to be a love–hate relationship going on but both partners can surprise us with their loyalty when the chips are down. Bonds can develop between cat and dog, born of adversity, that change their relationship for ever. One such tale involves a rather rotund grey and white cat called Dusty, belonging to another friend of mine. Dusty had been with Gill and her family for twelve years when a bouncy golden Labrador called Holly joined the household. Dusty was slightly appalled but chose the path of least resistance in order to deal with the new situation. She stuck her little nose in the air and just pretended the dog didn't exist. After a short period of curious sniffs Holly figured that the spherical grey furry thing wasn't that interesting after all and their parallel lives began.

This state of affairs continued until four years later when Dusty had a bit of a bad day. She often sunned herself on the cover of the large water butt by the garden shed. She decided that a few hours of soaking up the rays was as good a plan as any that morning so she jumped up to make herself comfortable on the wooden platform. Unfortunately it wasn't sitting quite right just then and the whole thing tilted up and deposited her in three feet of water before returning to its horizontal position as if nothing had happened. Nobody had seen her fall . . . except Holly.

Gill was preparing food in the kitchen when Holly rushed in, barking furiously and bouncing up and down. Gill had absolutely no idea that Dusty was in danger and probably going under for the third time (she wasn't built for swimming) so she was slightly irritated by Holly's insistent behaviour. She told her firmly that she couldn't play with her and to return to the garden. Gill had trained her dog well and she was confused when Holly continued to 'misbehave', rushing in and out of the kitchen, barking and looking behind her. Eventually Gill decided to follow to see what the fuss was all about. Holly led her straight to the water butt and it was then that Gill heard the faint splashing sounds of the sodden Dusty. The poor cat was swiftly removed and rushed to the kitchen for drying, TLC and a good cuddle. Holly had saved her life. Since then the relationship between Labrador and moggy has changed dramatically. They cannot pass in the hallway without a nose to nose greeting. Dusty curls up beside Holly in her bed and each stares adoringly into the other's eyes. Holly has become rather parental in her attitude towards the little grey and white cat and she can often be seen guarding Dusty, at a discreet distance, as the latter sleeps peacefully under the bushes in the garden.

I have had occasion a number of times throughout my career to marvel at the symbiotic nature of some inter-species relationships. A little three-legged ginger cat called Stumpy used to come into the surgery when I was working as a veterinary nurse. He came from a household with a very eclectic mix of residents, from Chinese Crested Dogs to African Grey Parrots, Persians and garter snakes. As an individual he was probably as nonchalant about all things furred and feathered as any of my friend Pete's eight cats. When Stumpy visited the practice for his annual check-up, the staff often remarked on the condition of his teeth. I remember asking on one occasion if he was eating dry food, since it is an accepted fact that this type of diet tends to delay the onset of plaque and tartar. The owner's reply was somewhat unexpected. 'Stumpy does eat some dry food,' she said, 'but I think it's the parrot that helps enormously.' Apparently the parrot, a free-flying member of the family with little regard for his cage, would approach Stumpy when he was resting and gently start to peck at his face. Stumpy would then roll onto his side with his mouth open and the parrot would while away an enjoyable few moments delicately extracting food particles from the teeth of his feline friend. Isn't nature brilliant?

One of my own personal favourites, probably since it represents such a contradiction, is the relationship that can exist between cats and rabbits. Despite the obvious hunter/prey potential it can be a rewarding friendship for both parties. Some years ago I used to own several rabbits. They had all been adopted from the local RSPCA after pressure to 'give them a good home'; rabbits are victims of neglect and cruelty in huge numbers but rarely make the headlines. Over the years I looked after Harvey and Pooka (members of an unwanted litter resulting from the union of two alleged 'females' according to the pet shop assistant), Mr Murphy and Elwood (abandoned in small hutches when their owners moved house) and Barrie (a fluffy Angora with unmanageable fur found matted and covered in maggots). Sadly, after some years, Pooka and Elwood died but Harvey, Mr Murphy and Barrie made the transition from outdoor rabbits (with vast hutches and runs) to part-time house bunnies. They were extraordinary creatures and I cannot tell you what pleasure and amusement they gave Peter and me. House training to a litter tray was a breeze; getting them to use the cat flap was a piece of cake. 'Why don't more people keep house rabbits? They are so user-friendly,' I thought – until I realized they planned to start a large house fire by chewing every electric cable in sight. We rectified this rather serious problem by putting casings over any exposed wires and refraining from leaving the rabbits unsupervised.

The point of this story is that I also shared my home with seven cats at the time. They were (and some of them still are) great hunters and part of their staple diet was young juicy rabbit. It may have appeared somewhat foolhardy to introduce food to the living room and expect the cats to resist the temptation of a nibble on an ear or two, but I had already watched the outdoor transition from food to family member as the cats became used to the rabbits' frolicking and general day-to-day activity. All my rabbits were well handled and sociable and I allowed the cats to enter their enclosed garden and get used to them. They seemed to understand perfectly that these rabbits were big, for a start (not quite such easy pickings); they didn't panic or freeze when they saw the cats and they smelt like me, to an extent. After a while I didn't see them as prey and predators at all.

Many an evening would be spent in domestic harmony; two humans, seven cats and three rabbits all cohabiting as some watched the television, some played, two slept and one rearranged sticks (Harvey had a thing about twigs and he spent hours picking them up and sorting them into parallel rows). I remember one evening with great fondness. My cat Bakewell, sadly no longer with us, was sitting on the sofa next to me with Barrie (the Angora rabbit with a harelip, ironically) propped against the cushions on his other side with his legs in the air and his belly exposed. This could so easily have been a recipe for disaster (or rabbit stew) but somehow I knew as Bakewell leant towards him that all would be well. With great determination my lovely black cat started to wash Barrie's impossibly long and scruffy fur; the mess of it all clearly offended him and he was attempting possibly to make order out of chaos. Barrie didn't seem to mind and continued to watch television, but Bakewell soon realized the error of his ways. After a matter of seconds he turned to me with a look of embarrassment and a mouthful of white fluff; if only he hadn't even started his act of kindness. Far too big an undertaking! A daft story, I know, but one that emphasizes how natural enemies can become friends in the right circumstances. It is, however, a tale with a big caveat attached to it. The situation worked for me and my cats but it is entirely possible that, given the appropriate conditions, something could have triggered an innate response in Bakewell and Barrie would have been no more. His size probably saved him; I wouldn't try it with dwarf rabbits. I would certainly not recommend that any cat and rabbit are left together without close supervision. The consequences could be too distressing for words.

However, I remember one occasion in veterinary practice when a certain lady, with the best of intentions, broke all the rules. She too had a house rabbit and a single cat and she introduced them carefully and at a safe distance. All went well, apart from the odd awkward pounce or two, so she considered that cat and rabbit were now the best of friends. The time came for them both to go to the vet's for their annual vaccinations, the cat for her flu and enteritis jab and the rabbit for his myxomatosis. The owner had a dilemma, however, since she only had one small wicker basket. But the problem was soon resolved, as we found out when she entered the surgery's waiting room with a very perplexed rabbit and cat squeezed into the same pet carrier. To this day I still do not know whether the look on their faces was one of embarrassment or horror. I would imagine that the trip was uneventful because both creatures had other things to think about. Please do not try this at home; just get a second basket.

I can only really give you my own experiences with interspecies relationships. Some work and some don't, but the important thing to remember is that different creatures' requirements may not necessarily be compatible. The obvious problem is the potential for damage should your cat become confused and suddenly see a family pet as dinner. I will therefore just pass on a few tips to ensure that the cohabitation is as safe and enjoyable as possible for all parties.

Fish and reptiles

Any creatures kept indoors in a tank could potentially be of interest to your cat, purely for the entertainment value. I would never recommend anyone to purchase a fish tank to entertain their cat, despite the fact that many find them fascinating. A responsible pet owner wants all their charges to be content both physically and emotionally, and contentment is probably rarely achieved by any fish or reptile that is stared at constantly by a slavering cat who repeatedly bashes the side of the glass. Most cats find snakes and lizards quite boring since their movement is usually languid and uninteresting, so there are rarely issues of intimidation. However, the tanks are warm and the allure of a hot spot cannot be underestimated. The most significant risk to any reptile is poor husbandry and, although I cannot categorically state that cats would traumatize them, I would want to discourage my cat from any potentially stressful attention to the tank.

- Cover any outdoor pond with netting.
- Ensure that tank covers are secure and that your cat can't comfortably use it as a warm resting place.
- Position tanks/vivaria in locations where your cat cannot make direct contact with the glass.
- Vivaria should ideally be situated in an area your cat doesn't frequent.
- All cleaning of vivaria should be undertaken in a secure environment *without* the cat present.
- Do not allow your cat access to any fish/reptile food or medicine.

Gerbils, hamsters, mice, rats, chinchillas, etc.

These are potentially the most vulnerable of all potential pets as their size and movement best mimic the cat's natural prey. Many of them *are* your cat's natural prey! It is just too much to ask your cat to respect the fact that this particular mouse is one of the family. Once again I would strongly recommend that any rodent is purchased for the right reasons and not just for entertainment value for the cat. Many small animals of this kind are kept in very poor conditions and half the fun of owning them is learning about their natural habitat and trying to create a simulated version in the domestic home. Any animal that is allowed to live in a near-natural environment will potentially be healthier than its less fortunate relations. Rodents will see the cat as a natural predator so, once again, allowing your cat to get up close and personal with your hamster is unfair. Don't be fooled into thinking that your cat isn't interested, either; many rodents are nocturnal so much of the intimidation may be taking place under cover of darkness, when you are asleep.

- Any exercising of your pet mouse/rat/hamster, etc. should take place under strict supervision and in a secure room. Your cat should definitely not be present no matter how trustworthy.
- Cages and pens should have a securely locked opening to prevent small hands or paws gaining entry.
- They should be located in an area your cat doesn't frequent – ideally in a place your cat cannot access directly.
- It is not good for your cat to sit on top of the cage in any circumstances!
- Cages and pens should be cleaned in a secure room away from your cat. Your mouse/rat/hamster, etc. should ideally be placed in a holding cage for their own safety.

Parrots and all caged birds

It is important to remember that birds are easily stressed and they can become ill or even die if subjected to a severe shock. Birds that cohabit with cats cope better if they are domestically bred and hand-reared rather than imported and wild. As in most cases, strange friendships can flourish if the creatures are raised together. Parrots are extremely intelligent and stimulating pets but they need as much attention as any cat or dog. They can cope very well with the presence of cats but early experience for both species is essential.

- Position the cage in an elevated location in the corner of the room to give the bird a sense of security; provide a covered section to the cage or vegetation for an added sense of camouflage.
- Ensure there are no clever routes that your cat can navigate to the cage (think Sylvester and Tweety Pie and you won't go far wrong).
- Ensure the door to the cage is secure at all times.
- Any exercise outside the cage should be undertaken in a safe environment without the cat present, no matter how nonchalant he appears about the whole thing. Accidents can happen.
- The bird/s should be kept safe when the cage or aviary is cleaned by being placed in a small secure holding cage. Exercise can be taken at this time in a safe environment *if*, once again, your cat is busy doing other things outside or in another part of the house.

Rabbits and guinea pigs

Guinea pigs can be kept indoors but they are not as popular as the up-and-coming house rabbit. Any advice given probably applies to both species since many owners still keep guinea pigs and rabbits together despite my suspicion that guinea pigs are better off with their own kind.

Cats and house rabbits

- Choose your new pet wisely if you intend to have a harmonious cat/rabbit relationship. The ideal companion would be a large, confident and sociable rabbit rather than a shy dwarf breed.
- Get your rabbit settled in a large indoor cage environment initially without exposing it to the resident cat.
- Once your rabbit seems settled and happy, your cat can enter the room and explore the new addition in its cage without risk of harm.
- The cage can be moved into other rooms where you intend to allow your rabbit but it's always wise to have established indoor quarters for sleeping (away from your cat) that your rabbit can access easily and quickly.
- Rabbits often approach cats, once they have a sense of their own territory, to establish who is boss. If your cat runs away (let's face it, some rabbits are huge) this is often enough to establish hierarchy in your rabbit's head and all will be well.
- Never leave them together unsupervised; despite the obvious hunter/prey relationship each species can do harm to the other.
- Cats soon acknowledge house rabbits as part of the social group and vice versa.

- Having house rabbits won't stop your cat hunting and bringing in wild rabbits for supper (unfortunately).

Cats and pet rabbits outdoors
- Rabbits need exercise runs in the garden but these should be covered to prevent your cat from getting into them.
- Teaching your cat that outdoor rabbits are part of the household takes longer since you spend less time with them and such rabbits are more likely to show normal responses to the presence of cats, especially if they are not exposed to particular individuals on a regular basis.
- Never leave them together unsupervised.

Dogs

I have thought for some years now that the perfect companion for a cat is a dog! Providing there is careful planning at the outset regarding the breed of dog there is every chance that harmony will reign and the cat will run rings round the dog for ever more. Many owners who completed the questionnaire for the 1995 Elderly Cat Survey spoke of the devotion between their dog and cat and the distress caused by the passing of one or the other.

Choice of dog
Puppies are easier to work with as they are young and malleable and will soon become used to the presence of another species, treating it as just another member of the family. Introducing an adult dog to an adult cat can be difficult since many dogs, confronted with a disappearing cat, will automatically give chase even if they have no intention of doing harm

should they catch it. If your cat has no experience of dogs this can be a distressing experience and many, given the opportunity, will leave home for a period of time before coming to terms with this drastic change in the household. The breed of dog chosen will also influence the future canine/feline relationship in your home. Terriers, greyhounds and other breeds designed to chase small furry objects would ideally be avoided – choosing one of these is probably just asking for trouble. The breeds that are traditionally considered good with children such as the Golden Labrador, Retriever or Cavalier King Charles Spaniel are probably sensible choices for multi-species living. Sadly they may well be persecuted mercilessly by the wily cat and have to give up their bed, water bowl and favourite sunny spot at the drop of a hat . . . letters from clients over the years have often revealed this tendency to torment. For example: *One of our neighbours got an Alsatian puppy not long after Tigger and Suki joined us – they terrorized him, stealing his bones from under his nose. They also used to ambush him when he was walked past our front garden, coming out from under different plants hissing and bog-brushed – so much so that from about nine months old the dog would not walk past our house.* And another classic example of the cat's ability to frustrate: *One of his main purposes in life seemed to be tormenting the dog belonging to our next-door neighbours. He would nonchalantly sit and wash for hours, right in front of their glass door, not taking the slightest bit of notice when the dog whipped himself into a frenzy of rage and frustration.* But genuinely good relationships can develop too.

Introducing a kitten to a dog

- Initial introduction is safest with the kitten inside a pen (these can be hired or purchased and measure approximately $3 \times 3 \times 3$ feet).

- Allow the dog to explore the kitten and vice versa without the risk of injury or a chase ensuing if the kitten runs.
- The pen can be moved into each room that the dog has access to.
- This process should continue for several weeks, particularly if your dog is protective over food, for example, and may respond aggressively when the kitten approaches his bowl.
- The kitten can be held near the dog with the dog on a lead to prevent chasing once both seem relaxed in each other's presence.
- Ensure the kitten is able to get away if he feels threatened.
- Treats can be given to the dog if he doesn't attempt to chase.

Introducing a puppy to a cat

- Ensure there are plenty of high resting places in the home where your cat can retreat away from the new arrival.
- Consider placing a baby gate at the bottom of your stairs to give your cat the sanctuary of the first floor.
- Introduce your puppy to his new home by using a puppy pen or crate.
- Plan ahead and start to feed your cat in an area away from the location where you intend to locate the puppy pen; this is to avoid your cat going off his food.
- Try to place the pen away from the thoroughfare leading to the cat flap or the normal exit route for your cat.
- If litter trays are provided indoors ensure they are located discreetly and in areas where your new puppy will not be able to go.
- Introduce the new puppy to your cat in a room where the cat can easily escape.
- Hold your puppy and allow your cat to approach, if willing.

- Your cat may hiss or growl but if you are holding the puppy you can protect him from any aggressive advances.
- Allow the cat to be in the room where the puppy's pen is located.
- When your puppy is out of the pen it would be advisable to keep a long lead on his collar to stop him from chasing your cat.
- Do not allow any unsupervised encounters until both parties are relaxed in the other's presence and the puppy has been trained not to chase.

Amber and Rascal – a cautionary tale

I don't see many cases where a dog is the root of the problem but it can happen. Amber was a pretty tabby and white cat and she lived with Debbie and her family in a town on the Sussex coast. Ever since she was a kitten she had shared her home with Maggie, the German Shepherd dog. Their relationship had been pretty good; Amber would use Maggie as a huge pillow and Maggie would eat Amber's food. It seemed to work very well. Sadly, Maggie died and the family were desperate to fill the void that she left with a little rescue dog. They eventually chose a medium-sized tan mongrel called Rascal, the decision swayed by the fact that the centre staff said he was very good with the cat that wandered in and out of the exercise yard. After a gentle introduction the relationship between Amber and Rascal seemed to be progressing nicely. Rascal became the perfect family pet and the children loved playing with him in the garden and generally fussing him.

After a couple of months something happened that shocked the family. Amber started to soil in the house, pooing behind the TV and peeing under the bed. She had always had a litter tray because she was kept in at night and Debbie couldn't understand why she was now so dirty when she had been so clean. Was she jealous of the attention Rascal was getting? Did she feel upset and rejected? Was she just using a horrible method to seek attention?

Debbie sought help from her vet, who referred her to me. When I visited it was clear that poor Amber had become a bit of a pariah in the family home. When I arrived she was sitting crouched at the top of the stairs with wide eyes as the children and Debbie played and laughed with Rascal. She was no longer allowed in the sitting room due to the heinous acts of the last few months and she knew her approaches would be rebuffed.

As our discussion progressed Amber quietly came into the hallway and Rascal's head lifted as he watched her progress. He was a good dog, he didn't chase her and the family reported that they seemed to be perfectly at ease with one another. He did tend to follow her around sometimes but Debbie felt this was no particular cause for concern. Amber just spent a little more time on top of the boiler in the kitchen. Nevertheless, poor Amber was depressed; as most cats are when they have to resort to urinating and defecating in places that normally wouldn't be considered appropriate. I had to find out why this was happening and I was starting to suspect that the not-so-innocent Rascal was behind her unacceptable behaviour.

Occasionally I am blessed with a gift piece of information from an unlikely source when I am trying to unravel the mysteries of a particular case. Little Ben (Debbie's youngest son) had taken rather a shine to me and he had been playing by my feet as I talked to his mother. When Debbie left the room to recharge the coffee pot, Ben tugged at my trouser leg to indicate he was about to say something that required my undivided attention. 'I don't let Rascal lick my face 'cos I saw him eating cat poo.' Good for Ben – not only was this a sound strategy, it was also the piece of the jigsaw that completed my puzzle. When Debbie returned I explained the situation.

Dogs love eating cat faeces. This may not be the most endearing feature of our canine friends but unfortunately it happens. Debbie had reported that Amber had turned her back on the litter tray and her usual flower beds in favour of the tiny spaces under the bed and behind the television. I would imagine that Rascal, in anticipation of a warm and tasty treat (sorry), pestered Amber mercilessly with slavering jowls as she attempted to use her normal facilities. This can have a profoundly aversive effect on a cat, hardly surprisingly, and it has to take steps to find secluded areas where the necessary bodily functions can be performed in peace. Amber did well to find two places where only she could go, but they weren't popular with the family, for obvious reasons.

The answer lay in finding safe and acceptable latrines for Amber that were out of bounds to Rascal. A small area at the bottom of the garden was duly fenced off with discreet bushes to shield Amber from prying eyes. Her litter tray was replaced with a shiny new one located within a cupboard with cat flap access. The soiled areas were cleaned and made inaccessible for Amber now she had comfortable alternatives.

We had one problem when Rascal nearly got his head shut in the cupboard cat flap but the provision of a magnetic flap and a little firm but fair training did the trick. Amber returned to acceptable toilet habits and was embraced once more into the bosom of her family.

❋　❋　❋

Multi-species households can work; cats are capable of forming bonds with most other species if there is something in it for them. I personally believe that cats are sometimes better off if they live with anything *but* another cat. It is, however, very tempting to presume that everything will be just fine and the cat will be able to suppress its natural instincts and distinguish between another member of the household and prey. If you adopt this attitude it may well end in tears. The answer is to enjoy the variety within your home, become knowledgeable about every species you share it with and think safety at all times – for everyone's sake!

CHAPTER 5

The Eternal Triangle

MANY OF US ARE TAKING LONGER TO FIND OUR IDEAL PARTNER these days. If we do take the plunge we divorce more readily and we are rapidly becoming a nation with a significant proportion of single people living alone. This does mean that we do our own thing and have our cats and everything's fine until, usually for romantic or financial reasons, we decide to embrace the concept of sharing again. By 2010 a staggering forty per cent of us will live alone, according to government forecasts. I don't personally think that all those single people will remain that way and as they need to adjust to considering the thoughts and feelings of another, so do their cats!

Oscar, Tabitha and Suki – more an infernal triangle

It would be far too simplistic to say that all eternal triangles involve 'girl plus cat meets boy'; life is rarely that straight-forward. Men really do like cats too, despite what *they* say, and I have been involved in many situations that resulted from the union of girl plus cat and boy plus cat. This can be interesting to say the least; Oscar's story is a typical example.

Oscar and Andrew had lived together for eight years. Andrew worked long hours and Oscar did his own thing but was always delighted when his companion returned to the safety of the home. Oscar was a bit of a worrier (rather than the warrior Andrew hoped he would be) and many altercations in the garden ended in tears, abscesses and a constantly decreasing sense of self-confidence. When Oscar was about four he decided that outdoors was just not for him so he made the choice to become agoraphobic. Andrew was unusually perceptive and tuned-in to Oscar's moods and feelings (it's rather an indictment of the male gender to say so but this is quite unusual) so he accepted his cat's choice and provided him with a discreet litter tray, toys and a scratching post. Four years of voluntary confinement followed until Andrew and his girlfriend, Sarah, decided to set up home together. They had met two years previously and were both delighted to learn they shared a common love of cats. Sarah had two six-year-old sisters called Tabitha and Suki and she took to Oscar immediately. He seemed so quiet and gentle; he wasn't exactly friendly with her but she presumed he was shy. He didn't respond very positively to her usual approach (cuddling, squeezing, stroking and kissing) but she reckoned she would win him round eventually.

Andrew and Sarah did discuss the potential implications of integrating two feline households into one, particularly as they were planning to move into Sarah's existing home initially, but they felt that Oscar was quiet and the girls were friendly enough and they would probably enjoy having a 'man' around the house. So the day arrived and Andrew and Oscar moved in. With the benefit of hindsight this clearly wasn't a perfect set-up. Sarah had been quietly oblivious of a rumbling tension between the two feline sisters. Suki was very much in charge; Tabitha stayed out of her way and attempted to go about her daily business with the minimum of fuss to avoid incurring the wrath of her sister. They both went outside but their chosen activities were very different, with Suki beating up everything in sight and Tabitha apologizing for her very existence to any cat prepared to listen. The last thing either of them really wanted was another cat wedged into the household; that would just complicate things.

The introduction was strained. Oscar retreated immediately to the apparent safety of a small gap behind the kitchen units and remained there, as far as Andrew could tell, for three days. When he did emerge, after much coaxing from his owner, his worst fears were soon realized – he had been transported into an environment that belonged to someone else and she was mean and feisty and would undoubtedly destroy him. Over the next few weeks the tension between the three cats was obvious. Tabitha and Suki started to fight actively and both females picked on Oscar whenever he could be found. He merely lurched from one hiding place to another, trying desperately to avoid his adversaries. The warfare was also psychological as the two sisters realized the significance of the newly acquired indoor toilet. They had both always gone outdoors but poor Oscar certainly wasn't going to explore the garden so his usual facility was installed in his new home. Tabitha started to use it immediately, realizing straight away how extremely safe and convenient an indoor toilet was. Suki saw its other potential and took to washing herself casually in the doorway, blocking all potential use by either her sister or the male interloper.

Oscar developed cystitis; hardly surprising really. Sarah and Andrew were still relatively unaware of the extent of the problem. They heard a bit of scrapping and growling but were things really that bad? Sarah did, however, take intense interest when two distinct things started to happen. Oscar began peeing all over the house and attacking her in the hallway and on the landing. If the urine wasn't enough he seriously meant business when he grabbed her ankles and poor Sarah didn't really like Oscar any more. She was frightened to come into her own house, there was a horrible smell and she was still trying to come to terms with sharing her home with another human being, let alone a ferocious and incontinent cat.

Sadly the relationship between Andrew and Sarah was a little ragged by the time I was called in. I spoke exclusively to Andrew since Sarah didn't want to know any more. 'It's your ****ing cat, you can deal with it!' she had said, apparently. I had hoped that both owners would have been there during my visit but quite understood the depth of the emotions that kept Sarah away. After many years of hassle-free pet ownership she had been confronted with a cat who wouldn't let her touch him, peed on the sofa and attacked her at every opportunity. Why would you put up with that? Andrew, on the other hand, was bereft. He loved Oscar dearly and saw a troubled soul rather than a naughty and unpleasant cat. We both agreed that he would concentrate on restoring his relationship with Sarah and I would see what I could do about the terrible trio.

New introductions into multi-cat households are often

difficult. When rumbling tensions already exist it can often exaggerate the problem and turn members of an established group against each other. In this case poor Oscar was clearly no match for Suki but the ease with which she could persecute him just made her do it more. Tray guarding is a common problem and a brilliant form of torture to those with a full bladder and Oscar's cystitis may well have occurred as a result of this (see my previous books *Cat Confidential* and *Cat Detective* for more details about stress and cystitis). Oscar couldn't go outside so peeing on the sofa or the bed where there was a soft surface and a smell of his security blanket, Andrew, was a logical alternative to the guarded tray. The aggression towards Sarah was another matter altogether. It didn't necessarily indicate that he held her totally responsible for his ill fortune but he would undoubtedly have been adrenalin-pumped and ready for action in such a tense atmosphere. Pouncing on her in narrow corridors may have seemed his only defence against an imminent attack; Sarah's response and subsequent fear reaction in his presence may well have prompted him to continue. After all, this was probably the first time he had actually made a successful assault on anything. I felt confident that if we resolved the cat issue then the rest would settle down automatically.

I devised a plan for Andrew that I hoped would alleviate the problem. We had to accept the fact that, confronted with the novelty of an indoor toilet, the girls would feel duty bound to use it or abuse it (Suki's guarding ploy). We therefore utilized the magic formula and introduced a further three trays in discreet locations. Andrew was worried that these additions would be firmly rejected by Sarah but I had to leave him to work on her and get her on our side. All these trays were an essential part of the treatment. Sadly it is rare that, once problems occur, things can ever return to the status quo. There is always a compromise and sometimes the solution to a problem can be a problem in itself. We continued with the programme and included more attention for Oscar from Andrew, play sessions (away from Tabitha and Suki's menacing glances), synthetic pheromones (available from veterinary practices) to give a sense of calm at a very fundamental level and the provision of several new private areas and high vantage points to enable Oscar to observe rather than join in the fracas. Before I left Sarah's house that day I asked Andrew if I could at least speak to her on the phone. I didn't feel comfortable asking her to do all this stuff if she was feeling so negative about the whole thing. I had a chat with her (I think she was pleased to feel she had a say in the matter) and explained the need to be moderately inconvenienced to restore harmony.

Andrew was determined to make it work; he was horribly torn between the two 'people' he loved most in the world, Sarah and Oscar. Immediately I left the house he was off to the local pet shop to bulk purchase trays, litter and toys. The introduction of the three new trays in the bathroom, hallway and spare bedroom had an immediate effect. All four trays were anointed regularly and the tension could be seen dissolving away from Oscar's face. Andrew loved him and played with him and Sarah was persuaded to feed him by hand with his favourite treat of ham. As each week went by Sarah became more upbeat. Oscar hadn't urinated anywhere that he shouldn't since my visit and he actually hadn't ambushed her either. She wasn't sure whether this was witchery or not but the reason behind Oscar's transformation was irrelevant to her. I tried to point out the power of multiple litter trays and a bit of play therapy but she wasn't at all sure I hadn't done something odd during my visit.

I cannot say that perfect harmony ever did reign in that household. Things settled down; Andrew and Sarah appeared to have resolved their differences and Oscar was definitely happier, but it was an enormous compromise for him. Tabitha ignored him and Suki could ban him from a room with one look, but it was a tolerable lifestyle. Should anyone in a similar situation ever ask me what to do, I would say plan ahead and take advice before you even try to combine two cat households into one, especially if one group is entering an established residence. Adjusting to the pleasures and pitfalls of co-habitation with another human being is tough enough without having to deal with the same issues in our pets' relationships.

Sandra meets Gary and Blue gets the hump

Sandra and her four-year-old grey cat, Blue, experienced a similar dilemma but the outcome was not quite so satisfying. Sandra had owned Blue from a tiny kitten and they had lived contentedly together ever since. She went to work and he went out to patrol his territory and visit his tabby friend, George, across the street (yes, occasionally cats do pal up). He would rest there awhile or stroll through the herbaceous borders until he heard the sound of Sandra's car. As she stepped out he would greet her by winding round her legs and pushing his head against her hands. She loved coming home to such a welcome. Blue comforted her when she was sad and de-stressed her when she was tense. Isn't this part of the reason we have cats when we live on our own? Three years into their relationship Sandra met and fell in love with Gary. Within the first twelve months they knew they were meant to be together and Gary moved in.

Blue had been wary of men ever since he was a kitten. Whenever Sandra had male visitors Blue would disappear out of the cat flap and only return once the man had gone. Sadly his reaction to Gary was no exception and on first sight he turned tail and thundered through the flap. The big problem was that, on this occasion, he didn't come back. He had taken an immediate dislike to Gary and Sandra had to trick him into returning home the following day. When Gary moved in, things went from bad to worse. He tried desperately hard to make friends with Blue (after all, the way to a woman's heart is through her cat) but this just made the poor grey cat wet himself in fear. Sandra even tried nailing shut the cat flap to force Blue to face his phobia but his paws became two claw hammers as he pulled out the nails, broke the cover to the flap and escaped in terror. The first few weeks of their time together in the same house consisted of a disconsolate Gary watching television on his own whilst Sandra crouched outside trying to coax Blue from under the conifers. Tears flowed and tension rose and they eventually agreed that the situation was becoming untenable. Blue had virtually moved in with George, his tabby friend, and Sandra felt as if she had gained a partner but lost a cat.

Before I visited Sandra we agreed that Gary would, temporarily, be banished from the house. A signal via Sandra's mobile phone would summon him home but the door would be opened by Sandra so he wouldn't use his key (Blue's signal for departure). I spent a pleasant hour with Sandra and Blue (tempted home with a few prawns) as we discussed their problem. He was a lovely cat, a little wary of me initially, but the lure of my magic bag soon had him rolling around the floor and looking generally chilled. Sandra was deeply distressed since her sense of divided loyalties was tearing her apart. She dreaded coming home and was finding everything very difficult to cope with. Unfortunately her mood was impacting on Blue, making him even more certain that Gary represented a major threat since his owner was apparently uptight about him too. In preparation for Gary's arrival we had barricaded the cat flap fairly comprehensively with a small chest of drawers, a large wicker picnic basket, a shoe rack and a box of vegetables (I wanted to test Blue's motivation to escape). I had spoken to Gary prior to his arrival and asked him to come into the room quietly with his eyes lowered and sit down on the chair. The phone call was made; Gary parked his car round the corner and walked towards the house. Sandra let him in and he entered exactly as instructed and sat down. Simultaneously, Blue jumped up and exited stage right, flinging the items blocking the flap in various directions as if he was frantically seeking bargains at a car-boot sale. Within thirty seconds he was out; that was a motivated cat!

Gary was a very willing participant in our therapy programme. He really wanted it to work since he could see the problem was almost driving a wedge between him and his lovely girlfriend. I asked Gary to enter the house in future as I had instructed during the consultation. He should initially talk in a whisper (he had a loud, deep voice naturally) and keep as still as possible, not making eye contact with Blue. Sandra had to relax so I asked if she could calm down since her anxiety was making Blue worse. A large wooden board was fitted to the back door to block the cat flap in such a way that Blue could not remove it in any circumstances, and this would stay in place for increasing periods of time to expose him to his enemy in a calm and positive atmosphere. Sandra played with him and gave him his favourite treats of cheese and Marmite, but only when Gary was in the room. One of the most important tasks for Sandra was to stop all the reassurance she had been giving Blue. Whenever Gary was at home she had fussed over Blue and comforted him constantly and it wasn't doing any good at all. She had to signal that time spent with Gary was safe and enjoyable.

Sandra and Gary followed the programme carefully over the next few weeks. Sandra did struggle with relaxing and she was a little despondent that Blue would still bolt through the flap as soon as the board was removed. Gary was also frustrated because he couldn't see that his efforts were reaping any benefits. However, after a couple of months they had a break-through. Blue started visiting Sandra in her bed whilst Gary was there. This was unheard of previously but, providing Gary remained horizontal and still, Blue seemed to be quite comfortable even if Gary wasn't. Blue had also spent fifteen minutes in the living room in his basket while Gary and Sandra were watching television. This was a triumph and things seemed to improve daily from that time forward. Regular telephone reports from Sandra were extremely positive and I almost put the file away with a big FIXED written on it. Sadly I hadn't predicted the complete mental aberration that poor Gary suffered the following week. He had returned home before Sandra to find Blue curled up in his basket. He was really pleased to see that the cat just got up and stretched lazily rather than disappearing immediately, and he felt an overwhelming surge of something that he was obviously unable to control. He walked towards Blue and tried to pick him up and give him a cuddle. He could have done no worse if he had taken a mallet and a chainsaw to him.

Blue panicked. He screamed and leapt out of Gary's arms, head-butting the wall hard in his frantic attempts to escape through the cat flap. Gary knew he was in trouble so called me first to tell me what he had done. Clearly he couldn't explain it as anything other than a moment of madness but the damage was done. We were at a very sensitive stage in the therapy programme. Blue was just beginning to redefine his opinion of Gary and was becoming more confident by the day. It was *not* the time to attempt physical contact, since the fragile relationship that was being created could shatter irrevocably with one false move. This one action sent Blue back to square one and beyond and his first response was to move in with George and not leave his friend's house for anything. Luckily Sandra and George's owners were good friends and at least he was in a safe place, but that didn't stop Sandra crying herself to sleep at the unfairness of it all.

Time went on and Sandra, bless her heart, persevered. She brought Blue home and Blue left again immediately he saw Gary. She almost reconciled herself to spending the next few years carrying her cat from one house to the other every day. Unfortunately the situation became more complicated when George's owners moved house. Their property had been for sale for some time but a cash buyer came along and suddenly things progressed very quickly. Sandra was concerned about Blue's losing his friend and the obvious confusion that her little grey cat would feel when he couldn't enter his sanctuary any more. She spoke to the new family when they arrived and explained her predicament and they gladly agreed to continue to allow Blue to come in. Their cat, Buttons, though, had other ideas and just wasn't having any of it. Blue subsequently spent most of his time under a hedge in the neighbour's garden or, worst of all, on the window sill looking into the house he used to call home. If Sandra tried to open the window and let him in he would run off. It broke her heart. It was time for the three of us to do some serious decision-making. We had to be sure that we were trying to keep Sandra, Gary and Blue together for the right reasons. All three were currently miserable: Blue missed George, Sandra missed Blue and Gary missed his happy stress-free girlfriend. I had a plan but I wasn't sure how Sandra would feel about it. I knew that all she really wanted now was for Blue to be happy. What if Blue and George could be together again? Sandra had already told me on a previous occasion that George's owners had reported that he was moping around in his new home and they suspected he was missing Blue. A couple of phone calls later George and Blue were reunited. Blue adjusted well to his new environment and was soon wandering round the garden and exploring his territory. Blue and George were often found in the evening washing each other or playing together.

I often think about this case because I don't believe I have ever worked with a cat so determined to hate one individual. I am absolutely convinced that Gary never harmed him in any way; Blue just took an instant dislike to him. It is sad that things were improving initially before the setback but I would guess that his firm resolve afterwards indicated the true nature of his feelings. Sandra visits Blue from time to time (always by herself) and she knows he's happy. She would desperately like to share her home with her boyfriend and a cat but she probably never will now after what happened to Blue. That's a shame, because she and Gary would provide a loving home, but you can see their point really.

Horace – sometimes they are not as upset as we think!

When couples come together, bringing their respective pets, it is always a slightly traumatic time. Will they get on? Will the resident cat leave home in disgust? Marion had recently acquired a lovely British Shorthair kitten. Her old cat, Tom, had died and she had always thought that having a pedigree would be wonderful. Tom was great but he had turned up as a stray and she always felt that he was very much his own cat. Maybe a pedigree would love her more? She called her kitten Horace and he moved in and all was going just fine. She knew she was spoiling him but he was worth it! He was very inquisitive and she spent the first few weeks rushing round after him, gasping when he tried to go up the chimney, panicking when he jumped on high surfaces and generally wrapping him in a thick layer of cotton wool to protect him from all life's dangers. She had already decided that the great outdoors was far too dangerous a place for such a sensitive soul. A couple of years went by and the bond between Horace and Marion was growing. He waited at the door for her to return from work, followed her everywhere and appeared to hang on her every word. Marion was delighted and felt that purchasing a pedigree had obviously been the right choice; he clearly loved her to bits. She did feel he was a little nervy and highly strung but she presumed that this was a result of his breeding.

Whilst Marion and Horace were getting to know each other there were developments in her romantic life. When Horace was about two years old, Marion's long-term boyfriend, Patrick, suddenly announced that he wanted to take their relationship to a greater level of commitment. He felt it was time for him to move in with Marion (bringing his dog with him, of course). Marion was delighted; it was exactly what she wanted to hear, but she worried about Horace. She wondered how he would cope with a big dog; admittedly Patch was ancient, slow and soft, but he probably looked terribly frightening. Marion spent many nights over the next few weeks lying awake with Horace curled up at her side, contemplating the future with some trepidation. The time came for Patrick to move in and Marion was full of mixed emotions. She was excited about living with her boyfriend but anxious that Horace wouldn't cope. The little cat got extra cuddles that morning.

Patrick arrived with Patch and the first encounter was encouraging. Horace had been brought up with a dog at the breeder's home so his first response was actually one of curiosity rather than fear. Still, Marion couldn't resist grabbing him every time he approached Patch and scooping him into her arms. When she had done this a couple of times Horace rushed off and hid under the bed, and Marion instantly felt that her little cat hated the intrusion. Two weeks later things hadn't really improved. Horace avoided the newcomers and, on the arrival of various items of furniture from Patrick's house, anointed a bed and a pile of books with a flood of urine. Marion was beside herself and I was called in to help Horace come to terms with his new situation.

I listened carefully to Marion's story and watched the young cat playing around his owner's feet. At one point he tentatively approached the fireplace and just as he started to sniff the chimney Marion leapt out of her seat and shouted, 'No, Horace, it's dangerous!' The cat flattened on the floor and looked terrified before being grabbed and squeezed by his owner. Patch came into the room (a dear old dog) and flopped in front of the fireplace. Marion's hold on Horace tightened as she watched him suspiciously.

There are times when we really can be victims of our own paranoia. Ever since Horace first arrived Marion had lavished intense protective care on the little kitten; she had assumed an air of extreme caution round her charge. Every time poor Horace attempted to explore and challenge himself in order to develop and grow emotionally, his efforts were thwarted. Eventually he learnt to be helpless and dependent on his owner to protect him from all these unseen dangers. He became tuned into Marion and responded to her every twitch and jump. He probably thought Patch looked like great fun initially but when he saw Marion's body language and her desire to protect him he feared the worst. When Patrick brought in the furniture and books with their challenging smells it all became too much for him, hence the breakdown of his previously exemplary toilet habits. Things had got on top of him.

I really didn't feel that Horace was bothered about Patrick *or* Patch. Patrick occasionally worked from home during the day and Horace seemed to enjoy the company. Patrick reported that Horace could often be found curled up beside Patch fast asleep when Marion was at work. The solution to this problem lay with Marion, not Horace. If she could bring herself to accept that Horace was perfectly capable of being in charge of his own life things would be vastly different. The little cat spent many hours gazing wistfully out of the kitchen window; he often rushed out of the back door when his owner wasn't looking only to be whisked back indoors by a panic-stricken Marion. They lived in a quiet cul-de-sac with a long and secure garden. What was the problem about allowing Horace the opportunity to explore the great outdoors? When I put that question to Marion she found it hard to find a suitable reply. I explained that if she backed off and allowed Horace to make his own decisions regarding what was and wasn't safe he would benefit enormously. I gave her details of appropriate products to clean the bed and suggested that she throw away the smelly books. She positioned two discreet litter trays in private areas (just in case Patch was a little too interested in the cat's toilet habits) to ensure that Horace always had a comfortable and safe place to eliminate indoors. And then I asked Marion to relax and let Horace explore his capabilities alone.

Over the next few weeks Marion was very brave. She introduced Horace to the garden; needless to say he took to it like a duck to water. She allowed Patch to sniff Horace and lick his head and didn't intervene when Horace climbed over him to get to the kitchen. Horace didn't have any more accidents and Marion soon realized that he had become less anxious as soon as she stopped fussing. She felt happier and Horace was clearly having a ball. As far as he was concerned the addition of one man and his dog was a bonus! A few months later I had to laugh when I opened a card from Marion and her family. There was a photograph inside showing Patch sitting in front of the fireplace staring intently at the empty hearth. Marion had circled something and on close inspection I could clearly see Horace's tail as the rest of his body disappeared up the chimney.

❊   ❊   ❊

I want to end this chapter with an honest confession. I am currently in the midst of a little turmoil with my own personal eternal triangle. Having resisted cohabitation for seven years (all great fun, I have to say) I have now met a man with whom I am happy to share my home. As I write we have been living together for several months but my dearest Mangus, my little Devon Rex, is not happy. Certain privileges have been curtailed since (how typical is this) Vicky has decided to fall for an ailurophobe who is also allergic to cats. I have spent the last few months following all my own advice: I don't force Mangus upon him nor do I remonstrate with him for his ridiculous and unfounded fear/dislike of cats. I have exercised the utmost patience whilst watching man and cat locked in a psychological battle for my affections. Mangus has learnt that, if she is very quick, she can lie across me in the evening in such a way that it is impossible for a third party to get anywhere near me without the risk of touching her. I sit pinned to the sofa with Mangus's tail in my face and her front legs spread across mine and I watch as they out-stare each other. Every now and then, when she catches him unawares, she licks his hand or face. This is guaranteed to endear her to me ('Oh, look at her, she likes you and she's trying to make friends') but send him rushing for hot water and soap. I am not that easily fooled but I think her shenanigans are working on him. Successes thus far include:

- he cleaned out Mangus's litter tray when I had flu
- he sneakily gave her a piece of his steak when he thought I wasn't looking
- he greets her before me when he comes in from work

What all of us cat lovers have to remember is that not everyone is made the same. You can be a good person and not 'get' cats because you just haven't had the personal experience of the joys of living with one. When an allergy is a problem then you are even less likely to indulge in pet ownership. All these people need is gentle, controlled and positive exposure to cats without someone screaming 'I told you so' when they start to succumb to the feline's obvious charms.

With all this in mind, my situation goes from strength to strength. He hasn't sneezed for some time now and recently he forgot to show complete disgust when Mangus licked him. He has read *Cat Confidential* (my first book) from cover to cover and I honestly think my little Devon Rex is grinding him down. Time will tell.

CHAPTER 6

How To Love Your Nervous Cat

I HAVE RECEIVED HUNDREDS OF CALLS OVER THE PAST TEN
years asking for advice about nervous or timid cats. All the
owners are experiencing problems with visits to the vet,
medicating and the general day-to-day practicalities of dealing
with a cat who will only be touched under very specific
conditions. These are the cats who won't be picked up and
whose response to approaches from humans is fuelled by
adrenalin; they either escape as far away as possible, freeze
(and occasionally wet themselves), or fight with teeth and
claws with or without prior warning. Even the latter group are
not aggressive cats by nature; they are scared and their chosen
strategy for dealing with such danger is to remove the obstacle

as swiftly and efficiently as possible. If you ever approach a cat who is low to the ground with its ears back and dilated pupils it is probably a very frightened pussy. If you ignore the warning you do so at your peril and merely reinforce the cat's belief that all humans are bad news.

Persistently timid cats are probably born that way to a degree. A cat's personality is a complicated mix of genetics and experience but if you are born scared the best early socialization in the world will probably still leave you hooked on routine as an adult and frightened of anything vaguely challenging. It is safe to say that the ones who hide from you are best avoided when you first go to view a litter of kittens, particularly if you are looking for a laid-back lap cat. The most significant period in a cat's behavioural development is between the ages of two and seven or eight weeks. If they are not exposed to positive contact with humans at this time (as is the case with most feral cats) they will grow to be suspicious of them and often extremely fearful. Given the right contact later, however, it is entirely possible to re-educate them to the delights of human company, providing a great deal of patience and careful handling is employed.

Whilst some are born that way other nervous cats are created over time by over-zealous or over-anxious owners. These are the ones who can be worked with and manipulated by changing the human's signalling and behaviour, which can have very rewarding outcomes for all concerned. However, even if your cat was born timid there are still strategies that can be adopted to make life as easy as possible. My own scaredy-cat Spooky lived with me for ten years after being rescued as a young adult from a local sanctuary. She was still scared of many things when she died but I can honestly say that the list was considerably shorter than when we first met.

Not all nervous cats benefit just from interactive changes. Some bypass the significance of the human/cat relationship totally and focus on the environment to fuel their fears and phobias. A letter I received several years ago from a cat owner perfectly illustrates the importance of the right environment to many individuals: *She was always very nervous and could never be persuaded to go outside. She never stayed in the same room as the family although she was quite affectionate with me. In fact, she has spent most of her life behind the boiler, under beds and in all other sorts of nooks and crannies she can find. The ring of the door bell signalling a visitor would have her dementedly looking for a safe place to hide! Yet ... since moving to our present house, three years ago, Twiggy has undergone major behavioural changes! She now stays in the same room (on the settee), almost tolerates visitors, is reluctant to move even when I vacuum and this summer has spent a great deal of time in the garden – asks to go out in fact.* If all else fails for you and your nervous cat you could always consider moving house!

The next few stories concern several aspects of nervousness; I hope they help by giving a better understanding of the pressure we sometimes put these cats under.

Daisy – a case of unrequited love

Lower urinary tract disease can become a real problem for persistently anxious cats. Some individuals seem to be predisposed to contracting cystitis when stress levels are high. Many progressive vets will now recommend appropriate diets and medication but also focus on behaviour therapy to address the necessary lifestyle changes. These problems usually occur in cycles so if stress triggers are removed it is possible to have a symptom-free life. I visited Daisy and her owner, Mark, for just this reason. Daisy was a little middle-aged black and white cat who had been diagnosed with idiopathic cystitis (this is a term used for a condition that is believed to be stress-related in combination with other factors) and was receiving the necessary treatment. Her major symptom had been blood in her urine but it was because she urinated on her owner's bed or on the carpet that the vet recommended a visit from me to see what was wrong with her world.

Mark was a lovely, enthusiastic and caring, if somewhat untidy, entomologist. He lived in a small two-bedroom flat with two friends, Tony and Brian. This did make things rather crowded but the sofa in the living room doubled up as a bed at the relevant times and they all seemed to rub along together without too much trouble. Daisy had lived in a number of places over the years since Mark left university and he had always felt that she adapted well. She spent most of her time asleep but she did enjoy attention from Mark, providing he waited for her to ask for it. He was very sympathetic to her needs and he had soon worked out that if he went to her he got a scratch; if she came to him the interaction was tender and meaningful. She had been suffering from cystitis, on and off, for a year and Mark knew when she was ill because she started to pee on his bed. During the consultation I asked to see his bedroom since I understood that all her physical needs (food, water, litter tray) were being met within this small room. Two things struck me when I entered his domain: first the smell and second that every available piece of floor space had been filled and I couldn't work out where my feet were supposed to go as I walked in. I asked Mark, as diplomatically as possible, how he coped with the eye-melting stench of ammonia from Daisy's indiscretions. Poor Mark had got to the stage where he couldn't smell it any more. I'm still not quite sure whether that is a good or a bad place to be if you ever have friends round but I accepted that, in the circumstances, Mark was fortunate.

When we left his bedroom, Mark added that there was another issue he would like advice on. Brian completely ignored Daisy and caused her no problems whatsoever but Tony was a big cat lover. Sadly Daisy hated Tony with a passion and attacked him on sight or peed on his bed whenever she got the chance. Could I make her like him more? Tony did actually appear at this point and explained that he constantly tried to talk to her and stroke her but ended up battered by paws and claws every single time. Daisy spent as little time as possible in the communal part of the flat, focusing instead on the crowded sanctuary that was Mark's bedroom.

Idiopathic cystitis is a relatively common problem in the modern cat and one discussed at some length in both my previous books, *Cat Confidential* and *Cat Detective*. The origins of the disease are still poorly understood but stress plays a significant role in triggering episodes of painful urination. Cat behaviour therapists work alongside veterinary surgeons to address the individual's specific hang-ups in an attempt to ensure that stress factors are kept to a minimum. When I am called upon to investigate these cases I tend to look at several predetermined aspects of the cat's life. Together with diet and lifestyle the most common problems are other cats, access to acceptable toilet facilities (indoors or out) and human/cat relationships. In Daisy's case we could discount the impact of other cats because she was fortunate enough to have a place of her own. The toilet facilities were certainly a problem. Mark had dutifully positioned a small tray in the only available space between the bedside table and the wall. In order to use this comfortably Daisy had to approach in first gear and leave in reverse or vice versa. There was no room to turn round or generally scrape about; yet the fact that it was full to bursting when I visited was testimony to her determination to use this unsuitable latrine as often as possible. The rest of the room was full with the bed, Daisy's food and water, a scratching post, Mark's shoes, CDs, books and dirty clothes. Hardly surprising that floor space was somewhat lacking or that Daisy found urinating on the bed more comfortable when her bladder was playing up. This was an obvious problem and one that needed sorting as soon as possible.

There was, however, another issue that I felt was causing Daisy some grief. I don't think we should ever underestimate the stress caused to cats by unwanted human attention. Many people just have to touch and hug all cats irrespective of whether or not the pleasure is mutual. Not all cats are made the same and some just don't understand the clumsy way we communicate. It can even be perceived as threatening, hence Daisy's defensive aggression whenever Tony approached and her avoidance of him whenever possible. Could this be as troubling for Daisy as her inadequate toilet facilities?

I discussed the problem diplomatically with Mark. It was clear that he had a great rapport with his cat and the relationship had blossomed because he had respected her personal space and her desire for solitude at times. He understood the limitations of his bedroom and acknowledged the fact that he had often seen Daisy backing out of the litter tray. He also mentioned that she cried and sniffed at it for a while and paced round before using it; quite understandable in the circumstances. I hate to come between a man and his bedroom clutter but things had to change. It was an accepted fact that Daisy needed to be catered for within the confines of his one room so drastic measures were required. I suggested the use of plastic storage containers and we devised a plan for some serious de-cluttering; it was not the first time that I have suggested a 'home makeover'. Minimalistic homes can be a nightmare for cats (so little stimulation) but there is a compromise between that and complete chaos. All Mark's stuff was placed in stacking boxes and arranged in a compact, albeit tall, column in the corner. The bedside table was removed and replaced with a shelf unit attached to the wall to house his alarm clock and various bits and pieces. Daisy's food bowl and water were placed on the deep window sill where she enjoyed sitting watching the road outside. This left the carpet exposed at the bottom of the bed for the very first time. We placed one new large open tray against the wall at the end of the bed and one in the original location. A nice fine-grain litter substrate replaced the original granules and the bedroom/Daisy's room was complete.

We then turned our attention to Tony, who was a little miffed that he had read the situation so badly and potentially caused Daisy so much angst. I asked him to ignore her for the agreed period of two weeks as an experiment to judge the impact of this lack of attention. If Daisy seemed to respond positively we would adopt it as a strategy for life. I was asking Tony to go about his business without talking to, touching or making eye contact with Daisy. If she should make a sociable approach (miracles do happen) he was asked to acknowledge her briefly and enjoy the opportunity to cohabit rather than manhandle.

I left the boys' flat with high hopes for Daisy's recovery. Mark, Tony and Brian were enthusiastic young men and they appeared to be taking the responsibility for Daisy's well-being extremely seriously. After two weeks I received a call from Mark to relate a miraculous improvement. Mark's bedroom had been transformed into an oasis of calm with spacious trays for Daisy's ablutions. The bedding, duvet and mattress had been cleaned according to my instructions to remove the offensive odour of past indiscretions. Tony and Brian reported that their eyes no longer watered as they passed Mark's door so I figured this was a good sign. Tony, in the meantime, had taken to his challenge well and had ignored Daisy completely. After a mere four days Daisy started to venture back into the living room and seemed content to sit some distance away from the boys observing their interaction. Since my visit Daisy had used both trays consistently and spent a great deal of time spinning round, digging and manoeuvring just for the hell of it.

It's impossible to judge how significant Tony's role was in Daisy's stress but it was quite clear that a change in behaviour coincided with a chilled and sociable cat. Daisy is still thriving in her tiny world with, as far as I know, no further urinary tract problems.

Saphie and Minnie – the nervous ferals

Andrea was a busy working woman in her early thirties who had always loved cats. When she left her family home she took her beloved Alfred, a tabby moggy of considerable stature, with her. He had been her constant and loyal companion for seven glorious years until, at the age of seventeen, he became ill and was peacefully put to sleep. Andrea was bereft; she had no idea how she would cope with the loss. She felt terribly alone but was completely unable to take in another cat since that would surely be an act of betrayal. Eventually, after two years, she decided that the time was right to look for further feline company. As a tribute to Alfred she wanted to give a home to a cat (or cats) who really needed a chance in life.

Maybe a little mite whom nobody wanted and would otherwise be neglected and face an uncertain future. She visited a local London cat charity that specialized in 'rehabilitating' feral cats. Andrea chose two sisters, ten-week-old kittens who had been captured together with a number of others from an area behind a disused building. Andrea was so motivated by her desire to rescue, reform and rehabilitate that she took little notice of the fact that she couldn't touch them. She also disregarded the hissing and spitting and wide-eyed look of fear from both of them as she stared at them through the bars of the cage; such was the nature of her conviction.

She took the kittens (now named Saphie and Minnie) home to her one-bedroom ground-floor flat with its pretty walled courtyard at the back. She had decided that it was best for the kittens to live exclusively indoors; that way she could protect them and nurture them and keep them from harm. Their first few weeks of life had been harsh and she felt that her flat would represent a safe haven of warmth and security. Sadly things did not go quite as expected when she got home. For two months the furry duo holed up behind her cupboard units in the kitchen. Quite how they found the impossibly small hole was a mystery to Andrea but she had to leave the entry point open because they only came out when she was out or fast asleep. She was beginning to feel that the rewards of feral rehabilitation were rather few and far between; she was spending a fortune on food and litter for two cats she never saw. Many of her friends suspected that she had been working too hard and the cats were merely a figment of her imagination.

After the first couple of months there was a breakthrough. Saphie and Minnie left the apparent sanctuary of the gap behind the kitchen cupboard in the early hours of one morning and moved their lair to the even smaller gap behind Andrea's bed. She was thrilled; this had to be a major step forward and an obvious gesture of trust towards their new custodian. I'm afraid I saw it rather more as the only other small and in-accessible place in the flat but I was happy to bow to Andrea's interpretation of that one. For a further six months they main-tained their routine of activity when Andrea was out (the evidence was everywhere that a good time was had by all when she was at work) or asleep in bed. The rest of the time they remained entwined behind the headboard. By the end of the first year both kittens (now well over a year old) were moving about the flat in Andrea's presence. They were, however, still jumping at the slightest sound and continuing to resist her advances. Saphie would just about tolerate a light touch under the chin when Andrea was lying quietly in bed but Minnie was not having any of it.

Andrea had made slow progress but she felt she had reached a plateau and she asked her vet for a referral to me to see if I could shed any light on her apparent failure. The first thing that struck me when I met Andrea was her enormous energy. She spoke extraordinarily rapidly and loudly and moved around her flat as if she was in an incredible hurry. By the end of the first hour in her presence I was feeling distinctly uptight myself. I saw nothing of Saphie and Minnie during my visit apart from a sneaky glimpse as I knelt on her bed and leant over the headboard. I always tell people not to disturb cats in their private hiding places but I made an exception that day; Andrea was keen for me to see how beautiful they were and she wasn't the sort of person to take no for an answer. None of her friends and visitors had ever seen the cats, apart from in photographs, so she really wanted me to be the first of many.

I praised Andrea's patience and tenacity in trying to resolve her dilemma but I felt that a new and different approach was needed to get the two sisters to the next level of their introduction to the delights of domestic life. The two cats had by now become accustomed to Andrea's presence. After a year this was inevitable. However, Andrea oozed anxiety with a slight hint of panic, and this must have created an atmosphere of constant tension and potential danger when she was around. If Andrea was frightened then the cats probably felt their best strategy was to remain behind the headboard until things quietened down. That is undoubtedly why she made the most positive progress when she was relaxed and lying in bed. Saphie and Minnie needed to experience more; they needed more input into their lives to challenge them and encourage them to do all the things cats should be doing. They were certainly entertaining themselves in the hours of darkness and when the house was empty but we needed to introduce some sort of activity that was so enjoyable they were even prepared to do it when Andrea was in the room.

I persuaded Andrea to invest in a system to secure her little walled courtyard. It was full of exciting plants and insects and would undoubtedly provide enormous stimulation for the two cats. Andrea had always been worried about the danger of the cats getting out and disappearing for good so this seemed like a compromise she could actually live with. We also talked about making them forage and explore for their biscuits rather than receiving them in a boring bowl. With the aid of forty-two cardboard toilet-roll tubes, donated by friends, family and colleagues, Andrea constructed two pyramid-shaped feeding units (the design is described in my previous book, *Cat Detective*). These would contain a random scattering of biscuits and each cat would then have to use their paws to extract the biscuits once discovered. This would entertain whilst promoting self-confidence when a meal was acquired as a result of their initiative and skill. We talked about a number of other sources of stimulation such as modular climbing centres, water features and toys but I was yet to discuss the most important element of the whole programme: Andrea herself. She really wasn't giving off the right vibes and if she wanted to communicate with them physically she needed to change her methodology. The insistent voice and staring eyes would have to go, together with the outstretched hands and the tendency to crawl towards them across the floor. We had to make her look so attractive that they would decide for themselves that she was completely irresistible and worthy of exploration.

I asked Andrea to take time out every evening to relax and meditate. It would not only be good for her as a stress-buster at the end of the day but the cats would find her demeanour much more endearing at these times. I told her to avoid direct eye contact or approaches and to speak in a softer and gentler voice. I suggested she call them 'beautiful' by accentuating all the syllables in a calm voice whilst slowly blinking her eyes. This word, for some reason, can have a hypnotic effect on some cats and I thought it might be a good discipline for Andrea to avoid her usual rapid-fire speech that the cats found so threatening. Special highly palatable titbits of ham or prawns would be used as a bribe to encourage approaches; Andrea was to introduce the concept of exciting and novel foods by placing small amounts in a bowl once a day. Once they appeared to relish the new experience, Andrea would sit or lie on the floor (or bed) with an outstretched open hand (containing a goody) and then stare into space in anticipation of a little furry mouth approaching and gobbling up the tasty treat. We would then build on this until they were brave enough to take the titbit directly from her hand in close proximity to her body. Play was another important part of the bonding process and I encouraged her to use fishing-rod toys to enable the game to be enjoyed at a safe distance.

Andrea was extremely encouraged that at last she had a plan that sounded hopeful. I went away and suggested she take a while to get all the new routines established and then call me for a chat. What a wonderful woman! She called me ten days later, having put into action all my recommendations, and her first report showed some early improvement. The courtyard had been secured and that very day she had allowed both cats out to explore in the evening. The previous owner of the flat had already installed a cat flap so I encouraged Andrea not to worry if she couldn't get them in. Propping the cat flap slightly open for a couple of days would be sufficient to teach them the entry point. All the play and feeding regimes had been adopted and Saphie had already taken a prawn from her flattened and outstretched hand (poor Andrea had lain there for a whole hour before she did).

By the fifth week Andrea had become fairly interesting at last. She had taken to the 'ignoring' stuff very well and she was delighted to report that both Saphie and Minnie had started sleeping on her bed. This was wonderful news and Andrea was overjoyed. I continued to support Andrea beyond the usual eight weeks because progress was being made on a weekly basis and I wasn't going to miss any of it! By the time we had got to the fifth month the two were going in and out of the courtyard constantly, being stroked by Andrea daily and continuing to sleep on her bed as a nightly ritual. As we agreed to part company since Andrea was happy to go it alone, the final report came through. Both Saphie and Minnie had come into the room when Andrea had a visitor as if they had been doing it all their lives.

I always feel that the task of taking on a feral cat is fraught with danger and complications. I'm not sure there is much in it for either party since a domestic life can be stressful for those not accustomed to the ways of humans or the sense of restriction. However, if the cats in question are young kittens, then, with a great deal of patience and gentle determination, they can make reasonable pets.

Sophocles and Demetrius – learning fear the Burmese way

Fear is contagious and few cases illustrate this point better than that of Sophocles and Demetrius. They were eighteen-month-old brothers: handsome, glossy chocolate Burmese. They lived with Jennifer and I visited them after she called me one afternoon to say she had the most dreadful problem. Sophocles and Demetrius had become shuddering wrecks, frightened of their own shadows. Jennifer didn't know what to do for the best; she couldn't understand why such confident youngsters should have become so nervous. Within a week of our conversation I was sitting in her living room being watched by the Burmese equivalent of CCTV as both boys sat hunched on the top of a tall bookcase surveying the mystery stranger in their midst. I tried to ignore them, since this would obviously be kinder than drawing attention to their safe observation point, and listened to Jennifer as she relayed the story of their gradual decline into fearfulness.

She lived in a large ground-floor apartment in a rambling Victorian building in a country village. The road leading to her home was relatively busy but a long sweeping drive approached the house and the rear of the building was surrounded by extensive grounds full of areas of lawn interspersed with thick mature shrubbery. Cat paradise, really, and Demetrius and Sophocles had enjoyed the first few months after their vaccinations frolicking in the undergrowth. Jennifer, however, was not happy. One of her neighbours had acquired a dog and she was most concerned that one day her boys would meet this beast with terrible consequences (and whilst Cocker Spaniels are not renowned for killing cats this was clearly a genuine concern for her). She began supervising their excursions outdoors and shepherding them around the garden with an eye constantly on her neighbour's doorway for signs of canine approach. After a while the cats started to pick up on their owner's vibes and became hesitant and twitchy; what was it exactly that she was so frightened of? After a couple of months Jennifer could stand it no more. She made the decision to keep her boys as indoor cats; after all, many breeders recommended this for their safety and well-being and the road outside was very busy and dogs are dangerous creatures . . .

Demetrius and Sophocles remained indoors for the next six months. They destroyed a bit of furniture, they became rather clingy towards Jennifer, but most of all they were vigilant and tense. Jennifer's new worry was how to stimulate them sufficiently to prevent boredom and she devoted a great deal of time and energy to entertaining them. Her demeanour within the flat became rather unusual to say the least. She didn't seem to relax; every day there was a need to ensure she was doing right by her beloved cats. A noisy neighbour coming down-stairs, mail coming through the letterbox or a telephone call would send all three of them into orbit. Jennifer was no fool and she realized something was very wrong. She decided to take a huge step and reintroduce the cats to the garden they had previously loved so much. She had actually met her neighbour's Cocker Spaniel on several occasions since the Burmeses' incarceration and she had been greatly reassured that he was completely harmless. She started to take the boys out on harnesses but the process wasn't particularly successful. She would step out of her door clutching both leads tightly in her hand, and walk slowly and carefully whilst constantly re-assuring the cats that all was well and each noise or movement was nothing to worry about. Demetrius and Sophocles, restrained and unable to escape any potential danger, dissolved into two heaps of frozen panic; Jennifer's reassurances merely confirming that danger lurked round every corner. This was not fun and Jennifer understood at this point that she needed help.

I was quick to confirm her suspicions, in the nicest way possible, that Sophocles and Demetrius's fear was a product of her behaviour. The Burmese had become dependent on her for stimulation, entertainment and security, as so often happens when cats are deprived of the ability to behave naturally. Her signals of tension meant danger to them and they were quite happy to hide behind her skirts until the big bad monster was gone.

The solution to this problem was very simple. Jennifer had to let go, relax and accept that the cats were perfectly capable of surviving without her intervention. They would probably, in the circumstances, cope more effectively if they didn't have one eye on their owner to gauge her response to any challenges. I suggested that Sophocles and Demetrius should be allowed outside (without the harnesses) for increasing periods of time every day. Jennifer could go with them but only if she could remain relaxed about the whole thing. She should avoid the temptation to comfort them if they rushed back indoors at the sight of something terrifyingly innocuous; they had to learn that Jennifer was no longer bothered. Cats are not stupid. Many times I have given the advice to 'relax' or 'appear confident' to owners, depending on the problem they are trying to manage. What I should really say is, 'Don't even bother unless you are truly relaxed or confident because you will be sussed immediately.' Owners don't realize that if they fake it they just look ridiculous to their pets (and to the trained eye of a cat behaviour counsellor!), appearing to walk and talk like a dodgy automaton. It has to be genuine and that can sometimes be extraordinarily tough.

Jennifer was made of strong stuff and she counselled herself quietly over the next few days to ensure she was *truly* relaxed before the boys ventured outdoors. She let them out first when teatime was approaching, always a good ploy to ensure they had half a mind on food rather than lengthy exploration of the great outdoors. She opened the door in an absent-minded fashion and casually deadheaded a few roses before sauntering in and awaiting the results of this first experiment. I'm sure I would have been proud of her had I been there. She spied on the cats discreetly through the kitchen window and watched as they crept from bush to bush with their bellies on the ground. Not exactly bold and brassy but it was a start. She shook the biscuit box shortly afterwards (she wasn't sure how long she would remain '*truly* relaxed') and the boys galloped in. They looked a little chunkier and more masculine that evening; Jennifer even described them as strutting around the flat for a change. It's amazing what a little bit of 'owner manipulation' will do to a cat's psyche! Sophocles and Demetrius (and Jennifer) went from strength to strength and all three are now happily and casually spending time outdoors at will. Jennifer has continued to encourage her cats to be self-reliant and they are blossoming into the cocky Burmese that they were always meant to be.

Flower – the cat who was scared of thunderstorms

There are several ways that we can get it wrong as owners of anxious cats; here is another example. Kathy and Andrew had a little cat called Flower; she was three years old when I met her. She had lived with the couple from a kitten but she had always been timid and jumpy. She had taken to Kathy immediately and often spent her waking time in her company. Andrew had fitted a cat flap to the back door so that she could go outside during the day when the couple were at work. Instead, she mainly chose to sleep during the day and get Kathy to open the back door in the evening so that she could have her constitutional. Kathy and Andrew began by shutting Flower into the spacious kitchen/diner at night but she started to scratch at the door and pick at the carpet. Kathy felt it was probably cruel to shut her in if she was unhappy so she got up one morning at 2 a.m. to let her out and never confined her again.

Flower had never liked storms or sudden noises and Kathy would always comfort her if she heard a loud bang. During storms she would rock Flower in her arms or cover her with a blanket to make her feel safe. A couple of months before my visit there had been a violent storm and Kathy had decided to take Flower into the bedroom with her and Andrew to comfort her. Since then Flower had gone to Kathy every night to tread up and down on her, miaow and purr and generally disrupt any sleep that was going on at the time. Kathy was worried about Andrew (he needed his sleep to function) and she ended up spending her nights on the sofa with Flower curled up on her chest to ensure that Andrew wasn't disturbed. Needless to say this was not a good strategy as Flower had started to get Kathy up several times in the night for entertainment, food or whatever took her fancy. It soon became clear why poor Kathy looked so tired. She would get up in the morning feeling terrible just as Flower settled down for a good day's sleep after a night of frenzied activity.

There were two problems here. First, Flower had a 'topsy-turvy' sleep/wake cycle that needed to change. Second (and most important), all that reassurance and comfort had turned Flower into a dependent creature totally reliant on Kathy for everything. Not content with being totally reliant on her owner she had also developed incredibly effective attention-seeking behaviour that turned Kathy into one enormous toy and source of entertainment. You can't blame Flower for being clever and working this out as a good strategy. We had to argue 'more fool Kathy' for giving in to it.

Kathy could see the error of her ways but she had the age-old notion that if she didn't do what Flower said then her little cat wouldn't love her any more. *This is a myth!* I bargained with Kathy and said that we would try it my way for a month and if it didn't work I would admit I was wrong. I did diplomatically point out that something had to change and we were actually stuck for any better ideas. The principle behind ignoring this type of attention-seeking behaviour is that succumbing to it isn't in the best interests of the cat. The more they get, the more they want, and it becomes quite stressful to keep pushing for extra (this is covered in more detail in Chapter 8). If Kathy withdrew from the relationship and encouraged Flower to be independent, things would definitely improve for everyone.

I asked Kathy to shut her bedroom door at night. We attached a spare piece of carpet to the area near the door so that any inevitable scratching could be ignored. Kathy and Andrew had to remain steadfast; any screaming for attention at night should be completely ignored. Relenting after several days because they couldn't stand it any more would be the worst thing that could happen. I suggested earplugs as an appropriate measure during the initial period of adjustment. The guest bedroom was made alluring with a radiator hammock and a small bowl of dry food to encourage Flower to rest in there for a change. Kathy would stop opening the back door for Flower and once again go through the cat flap training to ensure she got the message. Any storms in future would be completely ignored and Kathy and Andrew would go about their business as if nothing was happening. This is always a far more effective approach than reassurance; that merely shows the cat that she is perfectly right to be afraid.

A letter received eight weeks later read . . . *just to let you know that Flower is fine. She's used to the cat flap and has not bothered us at night. She also seems more confident. She spends a great deal of time outside and has lost some weight and is much more active.* It's amazing what a little healthy neglect can do.

❀   ❀   ❀

I will probably continue to receive countless calls about nervous cats. Things can be done, as you have seen, to make life as comfortable as possible but there will always be problems. Whenever I speak to owners I caution them about expecting too much from their charges. These leopards rarely change their spots completely.

Tackling anxiety by changing the relationship

- Do not make direct eye contact; view your cat out of the corner of your eye or under half-closed lids. Blinking slowly signals sociability and lack of aggressive intent.

- Avoid outstretched hands since, like a raised paw, this can appear threatening.
- Talk normally in the presence of your cat since hushed voices can signal your own tension and anxiety and these emotions are contagious.
- Speak to your cat in a gentle voice with a slightly higher pitch than normal.
- Use your voice in this way when producing food and interacting in a positive way.
- Avoid direct approaches since this signals a challenge and potential danger; even if you are just intending to walk past your cat, try to take a less direct route.
- Discover what motivates your cat (play, toys, food, titbits) and use these to create positive associations with you.
- Provide safe hiding places where your cat can seek sanctuary and don't disturb him whilst he is resting there.
- Do not reassure a nervous cat since this can reinforce the fear and make your cat too dependent on you as a minder.
- Touch your cat gently, initially for short periods during feeding or play. Avoid vulnerable areas such as the belly and legs at all costs and focus round the cheeks and chin initially.

The sad tale of Billy

Despite the fact that we are focusing on the benefits of changing our relationship with our cats when tackling nervousness I have to remind everyone of an important point. There is still no substitute for veterinary involvement since behaviour is all too often influenced by pain or disease. I want to tell you the sad story of Billy. Billy's owner, Angie, called me one evening last year, having been given my name and contact details by her vet. She was exceedingly upset because, subsequent to a visit to the local cattery, Billy's personality had changed dramatically. He was a seven-year-old moggy and he had previously been the model pet. He was confident and affectionate, playful and passive with the neighbour's cats, home-loving and talkative. He had a companion at home, Ted, a young neutered male, with whom he had a reasonable relationship. He hadn't been thrilled when the kitten arrived and had become a little quieter generally, but on the whole they played together, groomed each other and could often be found resting in close proximity to each other.

In January of that year the two cats had visited the cattery for one week whilst Angie and her husband went on holiday. When they collected the cats Angie noticed that Billy looked distinctly cross: his pupils were dilated and he was growling quietly. The couple just thought he was angry about being left, but when they got him home he was ravenously hungry yet too weak to jump onto the work surface in the kitchen. He seemed very nervous, so Angie took him to the veterinary clinic where they gave him antibiotics and a painkiller despite being rather nonplussed about the nature of his complaint. A blood test showed nothing diagnostic and by the end of the week Billy seemed to be more like his old self. Then, approximately a week later, he woke in the night in a very agitated state; he alerted Angie and her husband with his loud stressful cries and he appeared to be terrified, running round looking for places to hide in his frantic attempts to escape whatever was frightening him.

The veterinary practice recommended that they separate Ted from Billy as they felt that there must have been some social problems during their stay in the cattery. During the next two weeks Billy had good days and bad days; he would fluctuate between normal behaviour and apparent terror at the sight of Angie or her husband. He seemed to have lost all confidence in jumping up or down and he seemed clumsy. He even wet himself one morning when Angie approached him. Further blood tests for feline leukaemia virus (FeLV), feline immunodeficiency virus (FIV) and feline infectious peritonitis (FIP) all proved negative. Billy continued to miaow mournfully at the windows and his restless pacing was interspersed with moments of complete panic.

By the fourth week the finger of suspicion was still pointed at Billy's companion so Ted was placed in the cattery for a week to see if his removal impacted on Billy's state of mind. There was no significant change and his return a week later was met with curiosity rather than anything particularly negative. Week five saw a further deterioration as Billy urinated and defecated on sight of his owners. The vet had prescribed amitriptyline (a potent tricyclic-antidepressant) and Billy had seemed a little more alert and receptive to contact and affection. This was when I stepped in and, after careful examination of the facts, I was reluctant to accept that this was a behavioural problem. I informed Angie that I was on the case but wanted to discuss things with colleagues before committing her time and money to a behavioural consultation.

The man I always go to when confronted with this sort of case is a retired veterinary surgeon and practising pet behaviour counsellor called Robin Walker. The man is truly a genius and there is little he doesn't know, in my opinion. Having seen the history so far he set off down the road of a physiological rather than psychological diagnosis and mentioned a possible differential of Key-Gaskell syndrome (dysautonomia). This is a comparatively rare condition but I could certainly see where he was coming from. He also suggested trauma to the head causing a brain injury and I was of a similar opinion at that stage.

I persuaded Angie to see a specialist; I didn't want to delay any diagnosis by visiting and looking for behavioural moti-vation without checking all the medical options first. Billy continued to behave very strangely, waking her in the night and seeming to want her to follow him and then stopping at the top of the stairs and howling. The specialist did tests for liver function and blood parasites. He informed Angie that the next stage was an MRI scan. He had been worried about Billy's crouched movement; Angie had interpreted this as fear but it can also indicate a problem with the brain.

By week seven the vets were fluctuating between a neuro-logical and a behavioural diagnosis. Angie was still convinced that the kitten and the cattery stay were instrumental in Billy's current problem but as his condition deteriorated she was persuaded by one of the vets to sanction the MRI scan. Four days later Billy had the scan and, hey presto, a tumour approx-imately two inches in diameter was found behind his eye socket. The specialist felt sure that the condition was operable since the tumour was benign and very accessible. He had performed many such operations before so Angie took Billy to the surgery with high hopes for a complete recovery. Sadly, Billy didn't survive the surgery; the removal of the tumour went well but Billy never regained consciousness. I didn't meet Billy during the three weeks that I was involved in his case but his passing distressed me greatly. Sometimes it seems so logical that behavioural changes occur as a direct result of a bad experience. Fear in cats is always considered to be a valid response to danger, even if the threat is perceived rather than actual. However, in Billy's case the fear was mechanical, resulting from abnormal brain responses due to the pressure of the tumour. And the only really apparent symptom of his condition was the fear.

CHAPTER 7

How To Love Your Aggressive Cat

ANYONE WHO HAS NEVER EXPERIENCED CAT AGGRESSION AT first hand would be dismissive. They would marvel that anyone could be frightened or intimidated by such a small creature. There speaks the voice of ignorance; I have a healthy respect for all felines because I know they are capable of great things, regardless of their size. Nature has equipped the cat with a formidable arsenal of weapons. They have razor-sharp teeth in powerful jaws and claws that can disembowel a rabbit (nasty thought, but true). I have seen injuries inflicted on grown men that look more like the result of an argument with a lawnmower.

Aggression is very much part of the cat's survival strategy. It is required for feeding, defence of territory and sex. How naive of us to believe that we can wipe out such a fundamental drive just by inviting cats into our homes. To a certain extent we are acceptant of predatory behaviour and fighting with the neighbour's cat, and we usually neuter our pets so the sex thing ceases to be an issue. Why then are we surprised when they occasionally turn on us? The reason lies in our misunderstanding of the relationship.

Not all cats have had the benefit of a domestic upbringing where socialization has taken place at the earliest opportunity to enable the individual to form positive associations with humans. This learning process shows the kitten how humans express non-threatening sociability; we gaze longingly into its eyes, we embrace it and stroke it. To the uninitiated these acts of love appear to be nothing more than acts of aggression. They feel they have no alternative but to escape, freeze in abject terror or fight. Combine that basic misinterpretation of signals with a restricted and boring lifestyle and you have the recipe for disaster.

All is not lost since certain expressions of aggression from our cats are easily defused by changing our role in the owner/cat relationship. Following the simplest of rules and developing an understanding of feline etiquette will get the most amazing results. Here are three tales of owners and cats who, sadly, got it wrong.

Wickham – the wicked dictator in a leopard-skin coat

My first contact with Charlotte was a tearful and desperate telephone call. I should point out that she was the one who was crying but with hindsight, given my knowledge of the case now, it ought to have been me. All was not well in her house and she fretfully told me her sorry tale. She lived with her parents, John and Margaret, and an elderly Labrador called Fred. She had recently returned to the family home to live and she felt the need to have her very own pet that she could love and nurture. She had always been crazy about cats but she didn't want just 'any old thing'. She researched her breeds carefully and eventually decided on the Bengal as being the most suitable for her needs. She understood the breed to be sociable, outgoing, intelligent and dog-like. They are also blessed with the most extraordinary good looks so it wasn't difficult to fall in love with a young male kitten at a local breeder's home. She called him Wickham (she felt something 'Austen-esque' would be appropriate for someone so handsome) and brought him home. All went well and Charlotte, John, Margaret and Fred soon found themselves living with a rumbustious leopard-spotted bundle of energy and fun. He would leap on Fred's back, rugby-tackle human feet and survey his domain from the comfort of the top of the sitting room's velvet curtains. He had great entertainment value and friends and family would visit from far and wide to see him perform.

As he grew he started to venture outdoors and experience all the thrills and spills of neighbourly disputes and territorial spats. Charlotte and her family were vaguely amused to discover that, for all his energy and tough-guy behaviour indoors, he was the local wimp when it came to fighting. He would often burst through the cat flap at colossal speed to seek solace in Charlotte's arms as an angry tabby moggy pressed his face against the flap, only stopping short at the sight of the menacing large black Labrador within.

Charlotte couldn't really say when things started to go

wrong. However it happened, the household relationships had taken a sinister twist. Wickham's boisterous assertiveness indoors had changed into something far more menacing. The bouncing on Fred and the foot chewing had developed into genuine aggression, accompanied by a 'devil-cat' countenance that sent shivers down the spines of all who saw it. Fred had been threatened and intimidated to such an extent that he had been held against his will in the kitchen, afraid to venture anywhere for fear of injury from Wickham's teeth and claws. Every member of the family had at some stage been a victim of his controlling and malevolent behaviour. John and Margaret were unable to enter the kitchen without repeatedly feeding Wickham tasty snacks to avoid assault. The dog bed, best chair in the house, computer keyboard and anything else remotely significant in his eyes were now under his control. Wickham had achieved a *coup d'état* and Charlotte's household was now governed by a small spotted mammal.

I had visited many homes in my career which were being ruled with a rod of iron by the family cat. I had a healthy respect for such creatures (they really are scary) but an even healthier respect for my reputation as a fearless pioneer in the face of any feline dilemma. Whilst travelling to Charlotte's home I determined to let Wickham know that I wasn't taking any nonsense from him. Armed only with my trusty briefcase and a pair of stout ankle boots for protection, I entered the house.

My first sight of Wickham (purely from the corner of my eye; I wouldn't give him the satisfaction of an acknowledge-ment) was of a beautiful leopard-spotted creature lying curled up on an oversized bed by the radiator in the living room. I knew immediately that this used to be Fred's favourite spot. My heart melted as a sad black face peered through the glass door from the kitchen, almost pleading with me to return him to his rightful place in his soft, warm basket. Patience, Fred, patience. I sat down on a chair adjacent to the dog's old bed and explained to the family that, during the consultation and for a very good reason, I would not be acknowledging Wickham. I always feel it's important to point this out because nobody likes a stranger to appear dismissive of their pet.

As I took notes I watched Charlotte, John and Margaret as their eyes constantly flicked towards Wickham lying nonchalantly on his new throne. Then something happened. Wickham rose and stretched and looked across the room at John sitting in his favourite armchair. John immediately got up and walked slowly towards the fireplace, where he stood rather awkwardly with his hands thrust deep in his pockets. Wickham walked purposefully towards John's chair and jumped up. He circled a few times before flopping into the delightful embrace of a newly vacated warm cushion. I had to say something, so queried, 'John, what happened just then?' John replied that he knew Wickham wanted his seat since it had become his favourite chair and that if he hadn't relinquished ownership he would undoubtedly have been attacked. I was outraged. I walked confidently towards Wickham and gently but firmly pushed him off the chair. Wickham looked completely dumbfounded and was obviously too shocked to retaliate (fortunately). John, however, looked petrified and in the true tradition of any victim of cat bullying was extremely reluctant to re-establish himself in the chair for fear of future reprisals. I promised that I would protect him whilst I was there and that it was important he reclaimed his chair. Wickham returned to the dog bed and washed himself in a rather distracted fashion.

After much discussion I explained to Charlotte and her

family why their cat had become such a monster. Wickham had a very particular kind of personality; he was acutely aware of territory and the need to patrol and defend it outdoors. Sadly his attempts (unusually for a Bengal) were failing miserably and he often retreated to the comparative safety of the home for solace. However, another element of his character didn't really get the whole 'human-loves-cat-loves-human' thing. Everywhere he went within the house he was the focus of their attention. In cat parlance this spells trouble and he found it quite distressing, particularly once he matured socially and started to understand his role in life. In frustration he started to lash out and soon learnt that this actually enabled him to control the actions and movements of these annoying people. At least he could be boss at home even if he couldn't cut it outside. Contrary to his owners' opinion, though, Wickham wasn't that happy with this new regime and he constantly paced or sat with his tail swishing furiously. If only they would just leave him alone!

All the members of the family were listening carefully. I was delighted to have such an attentive audience so launched into a plan of action straight away. We had to return control to the mortgage payers and demote Wickham to the lowly position of family pet. Whilst this sounded great in theory there was the slight practical complication that all members of the household, including Fred, were terrified of said family pet. I explained that the key was attitude – positive mental attitude is the phrase, I believe. They had to sit, walk and talk with confidence and ignore Wickham's posturing and aggressive threats. If the confidence was there he wouldn't strike; cats only attack in these circumstances if they can safely predict the outcome. I had proved this time and time again when visiting aggressive cats but it is the hardest thing in the world to convince the owners that such defiance is in their best interests. We needed a secret weapon, something that would automatically make them feel brave. Margaret and Charlotte were horsy ladies with serious no-nonsense, nothing-scares-me attitudes when it came to all matters equine, so I encouraged them to adopt a similar approach to their relationship with Wickham. I emphasized the point that he wouldn't strike if they moved around the house as if he didn't exist and they seemed satisfied that I could be trusted. They promised to walk around with their heads high and a generally dismissive air of slight contempt for everything. It made them look a bit daft but it would work wonders.

John was a different matter. He had unfortunately adopted the persona of a particularly submissive Uriah Heep and his whole body language screamed apology and humility. He may have been a retired High Court judge but his demeanour now certainly didn't reflect such eminence. John was an intelligent and forceful character who had been completely deflated by a small spotted creature only twelve inches tall. I wouldn't dream of deriding him for it, since there but for the grace of God goes any one of us. He had been attacked and intimidated so many times that he couldn't even enter a room if Wickham didn't want him to. Advising him to be 'dismissive' just wouldn't work. I therefore suggested various techniques that might help him to feel more confident and less vulnerable to Wickham's inevitable attacks. We eventually agreed on shin pads, stout shoes and motorcycle gloves (anyone who has read *Cat Confidential* will probably remember my obsession with dressing my clients up in biker gear). This would prevent injury to the main target areas of John's legs and hands. I also suggested a regular feeding regime to avoid the need to give titbits, and various other symbolical gestures to ensure that Wickham got the message.

John was sitting quietly during the latter part of this discussion and I realized that something was worrying him. He felt he needed something a little more substantial than a shin pad or two to deal with the frightening scenario when Wickham came to the door of his study and blocked his exit. We settled on a devious plan. There was one thing within the house that Wickham feared: the vacuum cleaner. It was agreed that the appliance would be stored in John's study in future and any attempts by Wickham to block his exit would result in a sudden desire to do a bit of cleaning. This would undoubtedly take the wind out of Wickham's sails and send him running.

Four days went by and I received another tearful phone call from Charlotte. Things were not going well. I must admit I was shocked until I heard the reason. Her father had blatantly refused to do anything. He would not accept that shin pads and a more positive walk could have any impact on a cat who was clearly vicious. I was obviously mad or just plain stupid to believe that such simple and 'airy-fairy' actions would transform his wicked pet. And I thought he liked me! Charlotte was trying very hard and getting some results but Margaret, taking her lead from John, was continuing to behave exactly as before and bickering with her daughter every time the subject was broached. Even Fred was trying harder than his owners! I was stumped. How could I get them to at least try it my way? If it didn't work, *then* they could call me a fool! I asked Charlotte to have another gentle go at talking it through with her mother and suggested that Margaret give me a call.

I heard nothing for several days and made a note on the file that this was probably not going to work out particularly well without my terrier-like persistence and refusal to let go. I was going to have to be far more persuasive and make sure that they knew I wasn't giving up even if they were. I resolved to leave it a week before becoming proactive and making the phone call myself, but I didn't have to wait that long. On the sixth day I had a phone call from Margaret; John had been attacked again. Margaret and I had a long chat (John wouldn't come to the phone and I didn't press it) and we decided that enough was enough. Margaret finally relented and agreed that my methods were worth a try since everything they had done up to that point had been a resounding failure. I asked the six-million-dollar question – what about John? Margaret promised that she would persuade him by fair means or foul to follow the programme for at least a couple of weeks to see what happened. I was delighted; at last Wickham would be off the hook and able to relax in the knowledge that he was no longer the focus of everyone's attention. The initial frustration would be difficult for him because violent manipulation had been his modus operandi for some time. I was convinced, however, that he would soon learn to relax once he realized that the need for aggression had passed.

I held my breath and waited for the next report. It came a week later and included an interesting twist with an attempted Plan B from Wickham. Suddenly everyone was behaving differently and he was slightly wrong-pawed. Nobody seemed to notice his death stares any more and he was a little confused about his next course of action. A stroke of genius suddenly occurred and he directed his attention to the delicate porcelain and glass ornaments on the shelves in the living room. Surely walking clumsily amongst the Royal Doulton would get a response. It certainly did, and Margaret hurried across the room to rescue her cherished breakables. However (good old Margaret), his further attempt to get her into the kitchen now he had her attention failed. I was thrilled and explained to the family that the only reason he was targeting china and glass was his inability to get their attention any other way. So Wickham's Plan B simply showed that the family had regained the driving seat. The ornaments were immediately removed to the safety of a cupboard and the programme continued with renewed enthusiasm.

During the eighth week I received a phone call to say that a miracle had happened. (There was me thinking it was just an effective behaviour therapy programme!) Wickham had transformed into a quiet and relaxed Bengal. Once the initial frustration resulting from the shift of power had passed, he was able to breathe a sigh of relief and concentrate on being a cat doing his own thing. Fred now strutted his stuff and had regained control of the dog bed in the living room (dogs know when cats lose their edge). All the members of the family had become used to walking confidently and ignoring Wickham, who was now approaching them rather submissively from time to time for a rewarding stroke. John and Margaret admitted they had been wrong but, as I told them, it's hard to embrace the principle that something so dramatic can result from such small changes in behaviour. As we parted company at the end of our programme together I warned the family that they must not get complacent. Cats like Wickham are very beautiful and it's hard to resist the urge to touch, squeeze and stroke. If they reverted to their old 'look at the cute pussycat' ways then Wickham might well revert too. As far as I know he continues to behave impeccably. I wonder if John is still wearing those shin pads?

Whisper – the cat who was squeezed once too often

Monica called me about her cat Whisper. She was extremely distressed after a visit to her vet with her beloved moggy. She was convinced that he had a brain tumour or was extremely sick because he had done the unthinkable twice in one week. He had attacked Monica so viciously, on the first occasion, that she had been a prisoner in her own bathroom until her husband returned to rescue her that evening. She gave me a blow-by-blow account of the incident although, typically after such a frightening and shocking experience, I couldn't really get to grips with the actual facts. I wasn't entirely clear about what led up to the attack or indeed what happened afterwards; it was all a bit garbled. However, it was clear that he 'looked like the devil', 'went all bushed up' and 'screamed' before he lunged at her and bit her leg repeatedly. Nasty. The description of the second attack was equally confusing. He had rushed downstairs on sight of her and she had managed to escape back out of the front door as he slammed against it with his head in his attempts to get to her. More 'screaming' and 'devil eyes' accompanied this incident and he took a while to calm down sufficiently for her to feel safe to enter. The vet had given him a clean bill of health and, observing his apparently normal demeanour in between attacks, felt the problem was behavioural and a matter for me.

I visited Monica as soon as I possibly could, which was four days later. No further attacks had taken place since her phone call but she was staying vigilant. As I approached her driveway she greeted me cheerfully at the door and showed me into her tiny house. It had a small narrow lounge/diner and a separate and compact kitchen. Stairs in the hallway led to a bathroom and two small bedrooms. This may seem a deviation from the case in point but Whisper was an indoor cat and his world really was very small when I actually got to see it. Monica started to repeat her stories about the events but I carefully steered her away from this to go right back to the beginning. Almost all cat owners experiencing problems want to launch straight into the nitty gritty but I need to approach the case far more systematically. I need some background on the cat, the family and the lifestyle before I even start to talk about the reason for my visit.

In this particular instance I felt the clues to Whisper's terrifying behaviour would be revealed in the history-taking. I had my trusty consulting bag with me, full of exciting textures and smells and interesting toys. Whisper plunged in with relish and hooked out a small battered mouse that he proceeded to fling about the room with great gusto. Well, the gusto was as great as it could be in such a confined space; he did bump into a lot of furniture and stuff on the way. As we were talking I was making notes but it was all still a bit garbled, I'm afraid. The chronology didn't stack up and there were a host of contradictions. Monica and I just weren't talking the same language. Anyway, I persevered, but I started to get far more interested in what was going on in the room than what I was writing. Every time Whisper swept past Monica she would attempt to grab hold of him and squeeze him. 'Look, he loves it when I do this.' I begged to differ but only secretly. Whisper's efforts to complete his game were eventually thwarted and he ended up sitting on the back of Monica's chair with a lashing tail as she cooed lovingly and generally pulled him about.

I asked carefully why Monica didn't let Whisper outside and I was greeted with a fairly abrupt and irate response. Wasn't it obvious? She was a cat lover and, as such, she couldn't possibly expose him to the dangers of the great outdoors. There were other cats, cars going up and down her cul-de-sac, people, dogs and all sorts of other potential dangers. Honestly, what was I thinking? She did, however, take him outside on a harness into the garden to sniff the flowers. And it actually got worse. Monica had a lot of breakable ornaments in her living room and, during the day when she was at work, Whisper was shut into the hallway and upstairs.

We went through the details of the attacks again and I started to understand where Whisper was coming from. For the entire two and a half years of his life Whisper had been restricted in his activity. He had spent his time being loved to distraction by his owner. She hand fed him from her plate, she squeezed him, she slept with him and she carried him around upside down to prove how compliant he was and how relaxed in her company. When I asked her how often she played games with him she replied, 'Every day for at least half an hour.' I would never dream of calling a client a liar but I was totally convinced that this wasn't true. There was no evidence of fishing-rod toys or proper cat things and her body language told me she was merely telling me what I wanted to hear. Poor little Whisper had one toy, a knitted doll that he used to carry around in his mouth and repeatedly attack. He also used to 'make love' to this toy and I realized that Monica was using a euphemism for masturbation. Many neutered male cats indulge in this activity, using toys, bedding or items of their owner's clothing. Whilst somewhat unsavoury for many to consider, this hedonic behaviour often indicates a generally unsatisfying and frustrating existence. Thank God for the knitted doll, I say.

Monica pressed me once again for answers. Why did her lovely cat turn on her? I explained as carefully as I could that it was probably a symptom of a cat in crisis. Aggression is an essential tool for cats living a normal life. When cats are deprived of a natural outlet for this part of their nature it is almost inevitable that it will be redirected at some stage. All Whisper was allowed to do was exist within the confines of the relationship that Monica was having with him. This just wasn't enough. Many cats cope remarkably well when their natural behaviour is suppressed in an unsuitable and unstimulating environment. Others, like Whisper, become frustrated and chronic frustration can lead to explosive displays of intense emotion or 'rage'. Whatever caused Whisper to crack on that particular day will probably remain a mystery but his body whipped up a storm of adrenalin, his pupils dilated ('devil eyes'), his fur stood erect ('all bushed up') and he attacked as if under the influence of a 'red mist'. The second attack was probably provoked by an association between the intense emotion and the sight, sound or smell of Monica.

Once again I approached my discussion of the programme and hopeful solution with some trepidation. How could I tell Monica that her behaviour was squashing Whisper emotion-ally and that the aggressive attacks were an indication that things had to change dramatically? I started to explain to Monica how important it is for cats to be allowed to behave naturally and the dreaded glazed expression appeared on her face. If I know I am telling owners what they don't want to hear I immediately try another tack. I discussed the use of distraction and entertainment for Whisper outside the owner/cat relationship. I told Monica that this would allow him to 'let off steam' and stop targeting her in the future. We talked, negotiated and bartered about letting him outside but I was never going to win that particular battle. We eventually agreed on an outside enclosure attached to the house that would be accessed via a window in the kitchen. Whisper would then at least be able to feel the wind in his fur and take in the sights, sounds and smells of the ever-changing and exciting environment outside.

We continued to plan further interesting and challenging games for Whisper to play indoors. We introduced food foraging, cardboard-box towers and various other entertaining bits and pieces. I persuaded Monica to move her ornaments to the safety of a glass cabinet and allow Whisper into the whole of the house when she was out. At least that gave him a little more to do. I was now approaching the most crucial of the changes that needed to be made and that was to the relationship between Monica and Whisper. I explained that, despite the fact that he clearly loved her, Whisper needed time out from the relationship to be a cat. I encouraged her to play fishing-rod games with him every time she felt the urge to pick him up and dangle him upside down whilst kissing his belly. I wanted her to understand that love for a cat can be shown in many different ways and play was a very important 'I love you' message.

I left Whisper and Monica that afternoon with a little apprehension. I wasn't convinced that she had fully grasped the implications of *not* following the therapy programme, but I hoped that, after reading the written report I was planning to send her, she might finally agree that this really was the way forward for her.

Monica never reported freely after our consultation but I kept in touch with her. I couldn't abandon Whisper knowing that he was so unhappy. The outside enclosure was built and in use within three weeks and represented great progress. I am not convinced that Monica wasn't still squeezing Whisper and dangling him upside down but, luckily, he was so delighted with his outside enclosure that he was rarely indoors. A cat flap was fitted into a pane of glass in the kitchen window and Whisper often chose to spend nights on his wooden perch surveying his new nocturnal paradise. I asked Monica to keep in touch, but she didn't. Sometimes clients are happy just to get the results they want and don't feel the need to give the counsellor feedback. After my first call and with the knowledge that at least Whisper had his outdoor pen, I privately wished him well and filed the case notes.

Jeffrey – the cat who was loved too much

Every now and then you meet a patient and just know that that particular cat will be part of your caseload for ever. Jeffrey was such a cat. He belonged to a truly delightful lady called Paula and I first met him when he was just five months old. He was a magnificent example of the blue Burmese and as soon as I met him I knew he would be trouble. Paula had called me to her home to discuss various issues about her newly acquired kitten. Her long-term companion, a black and white moggy called Sparky, had recently passed away and she felt that he was going to be a hard act to follow. She couldn't imagine life without the company of a cat but she didn't feel that the average crossbreed would have half the character of her dear departed Sparky. She therefore did some careful research and came up with the perfect solution to her dilemma: a Burmese, described as 'dog-like', 'sociable', and 'highly intelligent'. What more could she want? So she found her nearest breeder and fell in love with Jeffrey at first sight.

She brought him home and fully expected a period of shyness as he became accustomed to his new environment.

Surprisingly he exited the cat basket like a rocket and proceeded to charge round her cosy little flat bouncing off walls,
climbing up curtains and generally behaving like a hooligan.
Paula was initially a little dismayed as she chased him to
retrieve the ornaments that fell in his wake. However, she felt
that he clearly had a huge personality and might just be the one
to replace her Sparky. Over the next couple of months she
tried to instil some discipline into his life; after all, she couldn't
let him trash the place every day. She said 'NO' when he
walked across the kitchen table and 'NO' when he scratched
the furniture and 'NO' when he climbed the curtains, but her
reprimands fell on deaf ears. She felt a little out of her depth so
she contacted her vet for my telephone number to see if I
would assist her in a rather preventative type of behaviour
therapy.

Paula greeted me like a long-lost friend when I arrived on
the appointed day and I immediately warmed to her. She sat
me down with a pot of tea and a selection of mouth-watering
biscuits and produced four sheets of A4 paper containing all
the questions and points she wished to discuss during our
meeting. I was thankful I had had the foresight to put four
hours' worth of money into the parking meter that day. The list
seemed endless: 'How do I stop him being destructive, how do
I get him to like opera, how often should I feed him, where is
the optimum location for his litter tray, should I let him outside
and if so should I get him a harness, how do I stop him biting
my friend . . . ?' I was writing copious notes as she talked but I
had to challenge that last query. I asked about the biting and
Paula told me that when her friend visited and they became
involved in a hearty debate on politics or current affairs,
Jeffrey would jump up and bite him. Another interesting point
about our initial conversation was Paula's tendency to credit

Jeffrey with incredible language skills. Words like V-E-T, C-H-I-C-K-E-N and M-O-U-S-E were all spelt out to me to ensure that Jeffrey didn't get the gist of the conversation. I had to concentrate to get the gist myself. We conversed for an hour or so and it became clear that Jeffrey was a lively, smart kitten with plenty of ways up his sleeve to run rings round Paula. He probably *could* understand each word and associate it with the appropriate experience; sadly his vocabulary didn't extend to the word NO. Shouting loudly merely entertained Jeffrey and the instruction behind the noise was lost in the sheer excitement.

I was keen to make things work for Paula but I remember quite clearly saying that day, 'Paula, I have to tell you, I think you will need my services again in the future for this little fellow.' At the time, I felt that the biting and generally boisterous behaviour was resulting from Jeffrey's intense need for 'input'. He needed to find out about his environment and understand his place in the world. Jeffrey was a bright cat and, given the undivided attention of the human in his life, he was making the most of an unnatural lot. He couldn't get out of the flat to experience all the excitement of outdoor pursuits so he worked the indoor environment as best he could. Every demand was met, even if the response was often not quite what he had in mind, except when Paula had visitors. When her attention was drawn towards others it wasn't long before Jeffrey realized that a strategically placed nip was not only fun but also a perfect tool for bringing the focus back to him.

We trawled through all her questions and requests for advice and we agreed to a little strategically placed double-sided sticky tape for the furniture and a plethora of scratching posts, Pavarotti at a slightly lower volume, dry food supplied via cardboard tubes and boxes, and a litter tray in a discreet corner of the bathroom. The issue of the great outdoors was a little more difficult to address. Paula and Sparky had enjoyed a beautiful relationship based on many years of mutual understanding. Sparky would go out hunting during the day and curl up on Paula's bed at night. Sometimes he would choose to do it the other way round when certain delicious prey was only available in the nocturnal hours. Paula didn't inflict her opinions and wishes on him and vice versa. She trusted him to return safely whenever he wished and had a comfortable understanding that he would come back unharmed because that was what he had always done. Suddenly, presented with a new little life ready to explore the hidden mysteries of the garden, Paula was nervous. What if he was eaten by a fox? What if next-door's terrier chased him? What if he got trapped in a vacant flat along the road? What if he found his way to the front of the property and the busy road? Paula panicked and, confronted with the enormous decision whether or not to expose Jeffrey to all this danger, chose not to. She had decided that a little harness-walking round the garden was quite enough to stimulate even the most inquisitive kitten. She had convinced herself that he was a hopeless creature with no strategies for survival whatsoever and much better off in the sanctuary of her tiny flat with the person who loved him more than anything. I did try to persuade her otherwise but she was becoming a little resistant to my coaxing so I decided to leave it to another day. I gave her some advice about protecting her visitor whilst ignoring Jeffrey's attention-seeking behaviour and promised to keep in touch regularly over the next few months to monitor his progress.

During that time I spoke to Paula frequently and used to look forward to our weekly chats. Jeffrey was making progress of sorts but my hidden agenda was to convince Paula that access to outdoors was very much the way forward for him. She must have raised every objection in the book and I must have come up with the most elaborate and persuasive reasons why her objections were unfounded. Eventually she relented and agreed that, between the hours of noon and four in the afternoon, Jeffrey would be allowed into the garden. She even very kindly sent me a photograph of him knee-deep in rough grass at the bottom of her garden to prove she was a lady of her word. It wasn't ideal to set a limit to his activity, and the time of day coincided with his usual afternoon nap. However, he soon realized that it was then or never and he changed his sleeping habits accordingly. He really was a very smart cat. By the end of our eight-week therapy programme Jeffrey had activity indoors and four hours of fun and frolics amongst the bedding plants. Paula wasn't brilliant about dealing with the attention-seeking behaviour – 'Are you sure it's right to ignore him, dear?' – but we came to a sort of compromise by arranging for her visitors to come between the hours of noon and four o'clock in the afternoon. If alternative plans were made Jeffrey was confined to the bedroom with a few tasty morsels, water, a litter tray and a host of soft toys. It was a compromise. The following Christmas I received a card from Paula and Jeffrey with a new photograph showing me how helpful he had been to his owner that summer when she was gardening. I don't think, looking back, I was fooled for one minute.

The following year I received the call I had been dreading. Jeffrey had attacked Paula savagely and she had received injuries to her right arm from teeth and claws. She wasn't in robust health at the best of times and I was concerned about her ability to cope with an assault from nasty bacteria lodged firmly under her skin. She was receiving antibiotics and said that she was okay, all things being equal. She also admitted that Jeffrey had done the same sort of thing two or three times before but not with such devastating results. Somehow she had managed to avoid injury up till now by pushing him away, but this time he caught her unawares. Typically, Paula was full of guilt, believing that Jeffrey's behaviour was purely her fault. She must have done something wrong for him to hate her so much. I agreed to visit her for a second time as a matter of urgency.

It was really good to see Paula again, such a lovely lady, but I was angry that it was under such circumstances. Had I let her down? Should I have been more forceful about my warnings for the future and her need to tone down the relationship? We spoke at some length and I watched Jeffrey, now a muscle-bound two-year-old, out of the corner of my eye. Paula was very concerned that I should remain safe and not be harmed by him; apparently she was not the only victim of his aggression. Both her cleaner and the vicar had been attacked on a number of occasions as they approached him to say hello. I assured her that I wasn't about to approach him to say anything, and the consultation continued.

The outdoor access had declined a little over the last year since Jeffrey started to bring in baby birds. Paula was a real bird lover and this distressed her so much she felt it would be best if he stayed indoors unless strictly supervised to prevent further nest-raiding. She did, however, compensate, or so she thought, by providing some intriguing and elaborate indoor games. I asked her to show me how she played with Jeffrey and she dutifully went to the 'T-O-Y-B-O-X' in the bedroom to get out the first example. This, apparently, was called 'Twizzlebonk' and consisted of a string with a ball made of wool attached to the end (the sort that used to be made with leftovers wound around cardboard rings). Paula proceeded to rotate this around Jeffrey's head in a wide circle (illustrating the 'twizzle' part) and he flattened himself on her bed with his head jerking frantically from side to side as he tried to focus on the whirling ball. Paula was stirring the string with great energy until finally Jeffrey launched himself (the 'bonk' bit, presumably) and brought it down. Truly exhausting even to watch; I was hesitant to ask what game would follow that. 'Rattytattat' was a multi-coloured cylindrical piece of heavy card wrapped with dyed rabbit fur in unpleasant fluorescent colours (completely irrelevant to Jeffrey but nauseating all the same). Paula proceeded to scream 'Rattyrattyratty' in a high-pitched squeak whilst leaning towards Jeffrey and waggling the weasel thing from side to side very rapidly. Her voice was achieving a banshee-like quality and I seriously contemplated grabbing 'Rattytattat' myself just to make it stop. Fortunately Jeffrey was on the case and, with a wiggle of his bottom and pupils as round and black as they could possibly become, pounced on the toy and proceeded to chew it and rake at it with his powerful back claws. Paula, with a nimble withdrawal, just managed to remove her hand in time to avoid laceration. I thanked Paula for demonstrating these favourite games so enthusiastically and asked if we could return to the quiet of the living room for a serious talk.

Jeffrey had turned into a little monster, not unassisted by the vigorous games involving a waving human arm. It was no coincidence that Jeffrey's 'attacks' targeted hands and arms. During our discussion it was also clear that he was becoming bored, destructive, frustrated and plain nasty when things weren't going his way. Paula, ever the dutiful owner, was falling over backwards trying to please him and failing dismally. We talked at some length and I was starting to feel the knot in the pit of my stomach that has become familiar to me over the years. It heralds that stressful moment when you realize no matter what you do, a particular cat is not right for the owner. I suggested letting him out again; Paula refused. Every trick I could think of to resolve this problem was going to be fraught with complications. Paula wanted a cat to love and squeeze. She wanted a companion to talk to and to keep her company in her little flat. Paula was lonely and all she wanted was a friend. Jeffrey wanted to hunt, to fight and to play with the leaves in the wind. This was not a union made in heaven. I had to tell her so I took a deep breath and said something like, 'You know, Paula, I'm not sure Jeffrey is the right cat for you. If you keep him permanently indoors I don't think I can ensure your safety.' She wasn't outraged by my comments but she used the one sentence that was guaranteed to get me right back on track: 'I don't think I could carry on living without him.' So we devised a plan.

This was not open to negotiation; Paula knew it was absolutely essential to get the programme right. One false move or a weakening resolve could potentially result in another attack. Paula *had* to stop focusing on Jeffrey, there could be no compromise. Since at least one of the previous attacks occurred in the bedroom I was concerned about the proximity of her face and vulnerable eyes when he grabbed her arm in bed, so he was banished from the bedroom at night. This was a major step for Paula but, bless her, she wanted to please me, since she understood how serious the situation was and how determined I had become to keep her safe. She finally agreed to allow him out again with fewer restrictions on his hours. He now had access to the garden during daylight and all her nesting boxes were given to a friend living nearby. I felt it was a good compromise to at least ensure he didn't have any more easy pickings. Twizzle and Rat were out of the picture and replaced with alternative toys on string attached to long sticks. We agreed on bamboo canes so long that Paula didn't even need to be in the same room whilst Jeffrey was charging after his twitching prey. Surely this would prevent his seeing arms and hands as fair game any longer? I promised Paula I would be on her case, because she *had* to change the relationship – for everyone's sake.

We spoke the following week and great progress was already being made. Paula was trying extremely hard but finding it very difficult to change her relationship with Jeffrey. She was absolutely strict about the new night-time ruling and, surprisingly, Jeffrey wasn't that bothered when the alternative facility was a brand-new heated cat bed in the living room. The bit that wasn't going right was the whole 'Jeffrey says jump, Paula says how high' arrangement that the couple had had for the past two years. Paula really felt that, since he was already deprived of his nocturnal cuddles, any further rejection was tantamount to cruelty. She had always kept up a continual dialogue throughout the day with Jeffrey, commenting on the weather, the news and the latest dramas on the soaps. I actually didn't mind that so much; I was more concerned about when this chatter was interrupted in response to a 'request' or an approach from Jeffrey. I just felt that if she was working on her computer and Jeffrey chose to sit on it at the same time she should move him off and finish what she was doing. That's not too unreasonable, is it? We needed to establish who was in control. Actually, what we needed to establish was something slightly different again. Jeffrey needed to understand that Paula was in control of her life and he was in control of his. This programme had to work; after all, if he attacked her again I would have to be *really* firm. Paula resolved to pull out all the stops.

The following week her routine report didn't come. I wasn't unduly worried because I felt sure that she would have contacted me had the worst happened. I hoped it was good news and this was confirmed the following week when she reported a real breakthrough. The previous evening she had been sending some emails, surfing the internet and working for some time on her computer. Normally, Jeffrey would have been outraged by her apparent lack of interest and interfered within minutes. She suddenly realized that she hadn't seen him for a while, and on investigation she found him idling away his time watching the world go by from the bedroom window sill. This may not sound like much but in fact it was progress indeed. At that moment Paula was in control of her life and Jeffrey was in control of his. There was a glimmer of hope.

From that point Jeffrey and Paula never looked back. I wouldn't say they drifted apart but they started to find interests and activities outside the confines of their relationship. Jeffrey would go out for the day and, despite initial trepidation, Paula accepted it was necessary for him to do his own thing. He always returned safely, just like Sparky. Jeffrey became more placid and calm indoors and the apparently unprovoked attacks ceased. In a way it's ironic that Paula resisted the notion of letting him out so much, seeing it as rejection and lack of care. Once persuaded, she was able to see that they both benefited emotionally and physically from the new regime.

Jeffrey and Paula are still together; their relationship has changed but they are much happier together than they have ever been before.

Bonzo – the guard cat

I have to relate Bonzo's story because it moved me greatly. Incidentally, he also ruined a perfectly decent pair of leather ankle boots, making the whole case less than cost-effective, but what the heck!

Bonzo was seven years old when I met him and a handsome, broad and masculine cat if ever I saw one. He also weighed 8 kg so he really wasn't the sort of cat you would want to have an argument with. His size was even more evident when you saw him in his own environment: a small one-bedroom apartment in central London. His owner, Judith, had adopted him as an eight-week-old kitten. Unfortunately, during the first year of Bonzo's life, Judith had become seriously ill and she spent long periods in bed, with friends and carers visiting to look after her. Bonzo was hugely supportive at this time as he rarely left her side and they formed a strong bond with each other. Judith gradually returned to good health and by the time Bonzo was two years old she was able to go out and start her life again. Whenever she came home Bonzo was delighted to see her and the relationship went from strength to strength. He had developed some interesting idiosyncrasies, mainly due to rather boisterous play conducted by several of Judith's male friends when he was young. As he grew to adulthood he believed it was incredibly good sport to swipe feet as they passed or hands that waved round on the arms of the sofa. Guests soon became aware of this habit and trained themselves to remain as still as possible to look less tempting.

Judith couldn't quite remember when things changed but malevolence had seeped into his interaction with strangers, and this had become a real problem over the years. He had started to challenge people as they entered the tiny flat. Initially this would be nothing more than a blocking of the narrow hallway and a hard determined stare. If the recipient of the warning did not heed it and continued to enter the flat Bonzo's next ploy involved laceration of feet and legs using a rotating, scything motion with both front paws. I had avoided this experience when I first entered the flat as Judith had wisely shut him into the bedroom, a confinement that he found deeply frustrating. After hearing the details of his attacks I couldn't resist seeing him in action myself. How frightening could a cat be, for goodness' sake? Unfortunately I knew the answer to that question all too well. I had often been the victim of feline attacks and I can say that my resolve is wobbly on occasions, particularly when the cat in question looks like a grumpy bull terrier. Judith let Bonzo out of the bedroom at my request and her cooing, lovey-dovey noises seemed somewhat incongruous when you saw the object of her affection. Yes, he was a handsome cat, but the expression on his face made it hard for anyone to instantly warm to him. He walked slowly towards me, staring intently, with his hindquarters slightly raised, his tail lowered and his neck stiffened. I continued to talk to Judith, at which point she became agitated. She informed me quickly that I really shouldn't ignore Bonzo because he didn't like that. I didn't actually like being stalked either but I explained to Judith that there was method in my madness. Over the next three or four minutes (it felt like an eternity) I was mauled several times by Bonzo with increasing intensity. I moved my consulting bag and he attacked my hand. I walked to the bathroom and he attacked my feet and legs. I was extremely tempted to stay in the bathroom indefinitely but I knew I had to come out eventually. My exit prompted the worst of all the attacks. He launched himself at me with great gusto, obviously believing that he had the advantage of surprise. He punched my feet and ankles so hard with his paws that I felt every blow. He howled like a banshee but still I walked back to my seat. I had seriously upset him but now I wanted him to calm down; I had discovered what I needed to know. I also only had half a boot left on each foot and I wasn't sure how much more punishment the leather could actually take.

Judith was shocked, since she had never witnessed such a severe attack before. She herded Bonzo back into the bedroom and sat down with me to discuss the problem.

Bonzo had become extremely attached to Judith over the years. He inhabited an incredibly small world in that tiny flat and everything within it had assumed huge significance, especially Judith. He relied on her totally for food, comfort, entertainment and companionship. In return he took on the role of defender of the realm. Cats have various ways of dealing with danger; Bonzo had adopted the fight-to-the-death strategy and was prepared to use violence to protect himself and Judith. The initial 'attacks' had been misplaced predatory behaviour but they may well have taught him an important lesson. Humans scream, flail their arms and eventually leave if you run at them and swipe them with your paws. It was also an exciting thing to do, representing probably the biggest adrenalin rush Bonzo had ever experienced.

The solution to this problem was a tricky one. Bonzo was locked into a cycle of behaviour that was closely associated with his current environment. The aim of behaviour therapy in this case would be to prevent further triggers for the attacks whilst promoting acceptable alternative activity that would be equally rewarding for him. This was my dilemma: what could I possibly do in such a small space? I also had another complicating issue. Judith was deeply emotionally attached to Bonzo and in order to modify his behaviour she would need to withdraw from the relationship and encourage self-reliance. She would also have to take some level of authority back from her cat. She used phrases such as 'he'd rather not be picked up', 'he doesn't like me doing that' and 'he wants me to do that at four in the morning, so I do!' Maybe this was why Bonzo felt such a burden of responsibility for his owner; she certainly didn't seem to be taking control. I suppose it's debatable whether or not cats are capable of such complex feelings. One thing I do know is that cats are control freaks, as I have said many times before. They are at their most content when they feel a sense of predictability and command over their surroundings and social situations. If Judith didn't appear to be in control then Bonzo may well have adopted this responsibility. However, rather than meet and greet friends and relatives as Judith would have done, Bonzo merely wanted to repel them.

We had many emotional discussions over the next few weeks. Judith was finding it very difficult to withdraw from Bonzo. I had suggested that she shut him into the bedroom when visitors came. I was seriously worried that she might adopt the strategy of never asking people round and I didn't feel this would address the underlying problem at all. For a short while she adopted my plan but lapsed soon after because she couldn't stand the plaintive crying from the bedroom as Bonzo objected to his confinement. Judith was unhappy and so was her cat and we just weren't making any headway. I had asked her to create some activity in the flat so that Bonzo could entertain himself foraging for food, climbing and exploring novel items. This was exciting for a while but Bonzo kept trying to return everything to the status quo. Why couldn't he just stick himself to Judith like he used to and get her to do all the stuff for him?

It is very hard to discuss these things with people. I really liked Judith and I understood everything she had been through in recent years with her illness and other difficult emotional upheavals and trauma. Bonzo gave her consistent and non-judgemental love whatever was happening in her life and however she was feeling. She didn't have to try to be loved, he did it unreservedly. If only he didn't attack everyone she wouldn't care how clingy he was. Unfortunately it is unfair to place this amount of emotional responsibility on a member of another species, particularly a cat. However much they seem to reciprocate love and affection in a human world it is hard for them to cope if they are not, to some extent at least, allowed to maintain a certain degree of 'cat-ness'. Yet Judith might feel that I was criticizing her or implying she was a bad owner if I explained this. I didn't want to make a depressed individual more so by removing the one thing that represented a degree of continuity in her disarranged life. We spoke at great length and after some time Judith said to me, 'Do you think Bonzo would be happier elsewhere?' This was a breakthrough and I was then able to talk to Judith about the possible implications of moving Bonzo to an environment with access to the great outdoors. I did explain that she didn't need to be out of the equation if Bonzo had a lot more to do. Wouldn't it be great if Judith could move house?

Our conversations over the next few weeks centred round this one theme. Could Judith pack up and walk away from London and make a new start in a rural idyll? It was a complicated situation since social isolation was the last thing that she wanted or needed at the time. If she were pushed into too rural a location she ran the risk of seriously compromising her quality of life, even if Bonzo was having a party. But Judith was becoming acutely aware, now she understood the situation better, that Bonzo was crying out for something (anything) outside their relationship. He would love to feel a breeze on his fur or damp grass underfoot; even a scrap with next-door's cat might have an exciting allure. Judith was racked with the conflicting emotions of love, guilt, resentment and frustration. It was a difficult time for her and there was very little I could do at that stage apart from listen and understand something of what she was going through.

Fortunately, as so often happens in life, fate intervened and along came Judith's cousin Lucy. Lucy had a smallholding in Suffolk and a no-nonsense attitude to animals. She had never met Bonzo but she had listened to his story with some interest. She had once remarked that what he needed was a 'jolly good hunting session in my hay barn'; an entirely accurate assessment in my view. Lucy suggested giving Bonzo a holiday. If he liked it there he could stay and Judith could visit frequently. Lucy figured it was probably the best solution for everyone.

So Bonzo and Judith went to Suffolk for a holiday. Judith returned and Bonzo stayed and is still there to this day. He has a few battle scars and he tends to go off for days at a time but he just looks right (all 8 kg of him) stalking along the hedgerows; he's even been nicknamed the Beast of Bury St Edmunds due to his rather larger than normal physique. The transition wasn't completely without problems; it was hard for him to totally redefine his concepts of space and activity but I always find that cats cope well once adjusted if they are returning to the lifestyle that nature intended. Judith visits regularly and Bonzo hasn't attacked anyone since. He loves to see Judith but he fits her into his busy schedule now rather than devoting huge amounts of time to her – which makes it much easier for her to leave Bonzo behind when she goes home.

❋ ❋ ❋

Wickham, Whisper, Jeffrey and Bonzo were all exhibiting aggression with differing motivations. The common theme, however, was relationships with their owners that needed to change. There is no question that their owners' emotional demands were of primary importance in the development of their aggression. It might have been born of frustration in Wickham's case due to the constant focus, putting him very much in the spotlight. Whisper and Jeffrey may have suffered from boredom and lack of stimulation resulting from their owners' inappropriate concern for their safety. Whatever the root cause it is perfectly clear that they were loved and cared for to the highest standards. The mistake many of us make is to view our furry friends as small people and see them as vulnerable child-like individuals who need us to provide emotional security. Sometimes we have to accept that cats always have and always will survive perfectly well without us.

Tackling aggression by changing the relationship

There is no substitute for professional pet behaviour counselling if your cat is being aggressive towards you or other humans. There are many motivations for this problem, including pain and disease, and it is essential to seek veterinary advice before trying any self-help approaches. There are, however, non-invasive changes that you can make to your behaviour around the cat that will minimize the risk of injury whilst professional help is sought.

• Avoid direct eye contact with your cat.

- Walk with confidence around your home whilst avoiding, whenever possible, a direct approach.
- Protect your vulnerable arms and legs if necessary by wearing stout clothing or gloves and boots; this will enable you to move around freely without being apprehensive.
- Avoid, whenever possible, passing your cat in narrow passageways or corridors.
- Ignore your cat and adopt the attitude that you are merely cohabiting.
- Don't put your cat 'in the spotlight'.
- Feed a dry formulation so that your cat can eat little and often throughout the day; this will avoid any frustration or aggressive episodes at mealtimes.
- Try to give your cat as natural a lifestyle as possible; access outdoors is always a benefit.
- Do not stretch out your hand to show affection.
- Acknowledge your cat only when he or she makes a friendly approach; even then only give brief physical contact.
- For safety reasons keep your cat out of the bedroom at night.

❖　❖　❖

I cannot end this chapter without providing an important let-out clause. Nowhere is it written that you should persevere with a pet cat who shows constant aggression towards you, your family or your friends. You can be the most conscientious and devoted cat owner and still make no impact on a cat that firmly lives by tooth and claw. Sometimes the relationship and the environment are just not right for that particular cat. Take professional advice and listen to it and don't feel remotely guilty for something that is not your fault. Human/cat relation-ships should be mutually pleasant and if you are being attacked and your cat feels the need to be the assailant then neither of you is happy.

CHAPTER 8

How To Love Your Dependent Cat

THIS CHAPTER TACKLES ONE OF THE MOST COMPLEX AND
fascinating elements of my work as a cat behaviour counsellor.
What happens when a relationship between human and cat
oversteps the boundary of what is considered 'normal'? What
actually constitutes a dysfunctional relationship and why are
they so undesirable? I have therefore decided to group
together a number of issues that relate to this topic. I want to
look not only at dependent cats but dependent humans: people
who have intensely emotional attachments to their cats. These
attachments are wonderful on a certain level but they can
become extremely distressing when the cat dies or becomes ill.
They can also be experienced to the exclusion of other humans

and whilst some people would argue 'Who needs a human when you have a loving cat?' I feel slightly uneasy about this. I have always suggested as diplomatically as possible that cats are ill equipped to reciprocate in these intense relationships; maybe some of the problems illustrated in the next few stories will back up my reservations.

I also want to discuss attention-seeking behaviour. This manifests itself in (what appears to be) wilful manipulation of the owner by a cynical little cat with nothing better to do with his time than get the owner up at three o'clock in the morning to heat up some prawns, *just because he can!* I will admit this can be extremely amusing and entertaining until it happens to you. It can also be detrimental to the emotional health of the cat, who becomes too dependent on the owner for interaction and very uptight because the more he demands, the more he wants.

Rob and Flossie

Over-attached relationships are not always the domain of the female. Men also often live alone and work long hours and coming home to a warm welcome from a cat is as important to them as it is to us women. There are many books available that tell us that men come from a different planet and their brains just don't work the same way as ours. It is certainly true that in my experience a cat could enter a room and do a complicated song-and-dance routine complete with cane and top hat, and most men would be oblivious if watching the television. Attention-seeking behaviour rarely works in those circum-stances. However, this is not to say that some men do not have the ability to multi-task or to understand the subtle nuances of their cats' behaviour. Some men are also keen to please their cats and provide everything they need to make them happy. Rob was such a man and a nicer client you couldn't wish to meet.

Rob had left university and set up home alone with a good job in a strange town. He had muddled along relatively well for a couple of years but realized there was something missing in his life. His family had always had cats when he was growing up and he remembered with fondness how each individual had helped him through difficult times with exams, girlfriends and all the tribulations of growing up. He felt his life would be greatly enhanced if he took the plunge and acquired a cat from the local rescue centre.

Rob was a bit of a softie and taking a softie into a rescue cattery virtually guarantees that at least seven will leave with him or her. However, he was after all a man and the rational part of his brain took over and chose one small black cat. She had belonged to an elderly lady who had died and she sat in her cage looking dishevelled and unloved. Rob reached in to pick her up and her purr in anticipation melted his heart. Her subsequent scratch to his arm when he held her for just a little too long sealed it for him and he signed the adoption paperwork and took her home. This was for life!

Rob wanted to do everything to guarantee Flossie's comfort and safety. After all, she'd lost her previous owner and was probably mourning; she needed cheering up. He fitted a cat flap to the back door to give access to the garden and he provided her with the best food that money could buy. All was going really well until they suffered their first invasion. Rob had just said goodnight to Flossie in the living room and retired to bed. When he found himself saying goodnight to Flossie again under his bedside table he realized something was wrong. He chased the interloper out of the house and thought nothing more of it until a big black and white cat started the same trick. This had to stop since it was obviously distressing Flossie. She had developed the unfortunate habit of regurgitating her food if she saw this cat through the window or heard him banging at the cat flap. Rob thought she might be ill but veterinary examination could not find a definitive cause for her parting company with her breakfast so consistently. He was determined to restore Flossie's sanctuary so he shut the cat flap and provided her with a litter tray. If she wasn't safe outside then she would have to stay in.

Rob spent unhappy evenings watching Flossie wince every time the black and white cat bashed at the cat flap trying to break in. He was really worried, because he could see that she was deteriorating. Her coat became unkempt and she seemed to rely heavily on him. If he passed her sitting on the sofa she would squeal at him and only settle if he sat down and provided her with the warmth and security of his lap. He was almost getting to the stage when he couldn't do anything at home apart from provide comfort to his cat. His chores were left unfinished and he gave every moment to Flossie when he was at home. It seemed to help for a while, particularly when he took a week off work, but as soon as he went back Flossie panicked. That very evening Rob returned to find a wet patch of urine on his sofa and a little black cat desperate for a fuss.

Poor Rob had very mixed emotions because he started to blame himself. He felt that this 'dirty protest' was a direct result of his depriving her of his company. He should never have given her all of him and then taken it away. It was cruel in the extreme and he should have predicted the response. What was the answer? Try to get the bosses to allow him to work more from home? Employ a cat-sitter? Give up work completely and become a permanent carer for Flossie? Whilst none of these options was seriously considered a thousand things were going through Rob's head when he rang me to arrange a visit. Flossie had continued to soil on the sofa and regurgitate her food and her overall condition was suffering. She looked older than her years and all she wanted to do was sleep (preferably on Rob's lap) or cling to him and howl when awake. He felt wretched every time he went to work and he even felt his own health was suffering as a result. He couldn't wait to get home but secretly dreaded the immense responsibility of being everything to Flossie.

I spent a couple of hours with Rob and Flossie going through the events that had led to the current situation. Flossie truly was a dear little thing and she watched Rob's every move like a devoted hawk. Her dreamy gaze was withdrawn every now and then as her glance flickered between the door to the kitchen and the living-room window. What was she hearing? What was she afraid of? Rob had reported that she seemed keen to go outside but merely sat on the step and cried when she did so. After an hour the sight of a big black and white face at the living-room window confirmed my suspicions. Flossie's main concern was out there. It was certainly true that her owner had tied himself in knots and ended up with a dependent cat, but the primary cause of her dependency was lack of security brought on by other cats, not Rob's behaviour. I think it was an enormous relief to Rob to know that it wasn't he who had screwed her up.

We talked about the three main problems at some length, namely the regurgitation, the soiling and the apparent dependency. We also discussed the main cause – the black and white cat and all his pals outside who were keen to take over the domain of the new little black cat on the block. A pattern started to emerge when we discussed the regurgitation of her food. It didn't happen after every meal but it would definitely occur if she had seen the cat outside the window, heard a bash at the cat flap whilst eating or been deprived of Rob's company after a period when he had been at home. Could it be stress-related? Her urination pattern on the sofa seemed to follow a similar trend. We had to create a situation that would increase Flossie's sense of security in the home without Rob's having to leave his job and take permanent responsibility. In the long run dependencies are never in anyone's interest since twenty-four-hour preoccupation with our pets is rarely an option (and even if it were I truly wouldn't recommend it). If we become indispensable to our furry friends then every time we try to leave them it is incredibly distressing for all concerned. It would be a far better strategy to prevent it from happening in the first place.

I asked Rob to block up the cat flap on both sides. Locking a flap just doesn't deter potential invaders; they just bang on it and keep returning until it breaks or some fool unlocks it. If the cat flap suddenly disappears one day (a big sheet of plywood will do it) then it no longer represents a weak point in the defences of the home. Cue for big black and white cat to move on to another target elsewhere in the street. Flossie still had a strong urge to go outside, which seems to be relatively common in such cases – these poor persecuted individuals don't particularly want to bump into their enemy but they feel compelled to check the territory daily to see what they have been up to. Flossie clearly couldn't do this alone but she might like to take a constitutional if Rob was in the garden. I wasn't condoning Rob's role as her minder but his presence in the garden, occupied with other things, might give her the confidence she needed to make her mark in the garden and check for the whereabouts of you-know-who.

Flossie was not a young cat (despite the rescue centre's referring to her as 'adult, probably about five years old'). I felt she was at least double that and with her advancing years came all the insecurities that go hand in hand with old age. She needed somewhere warm to sleep that was a suitable alternative to Rob's lap. If he wasn't responding to her plaintive cry for him to sit down and provide a bed maybe she would take to something else? We decided on a piece of synthetic sheepskin that would be spread over the sofa (on the as yet unblemished part of the seat) to tempt her. Rob was instructed to purchase various toys that I felt Flossie would find irresistible. Their interaction would in future focus on predatory play rather than cuddles and strokes. Whilst cuddling was great it didn't do anything but confirm Rob's status as nurturer and comforter. That wasn't really what we were after at that moment.

Rob agreed to groom Flossie more often to keep her coat as well maintained as possible. She had given up grooming since all this started and she was looking a little moth-eaten. That would enable Rob and Flossie to have bouts of the physical contact that they both clearly enjoyed with the more positive end result of a glossy coat. Various other recommendations were made such as an additional litter tray away from any windows and a change to a fine sand-like litter material. I also suggested that Rob follow a 'little and often' approach to feeding so that Flossie couldn't take too much food down at once on a stressed stomach. With the aid of a couple of automatic feeders, Flossie would have four meals a day instead of two from then on.

Over the next eight weeks we saw a great improvement in Flossie. She seemed to have more life in her and a definite spring in her step. She took to her thermal sheepskin bed immediately and she was found curled up and toasty every evening when Rob came home. The blocking of the cat flap seemed to provide her with a symbolical gesture of security. Rob's lap wasn't as essential as before for deep relaxed sleep now that the risk of invasion had seriously diminished. Play sessions were fun exercise and a valuable distraction for Flossie from all the worries of defending her home. If the weather was pleasant excursions into the garden took place during the evening and at weekends and Rob discovered the stress-busting delights of pottering in his garden.

Unfortunately there were continuing spates of peeing on the sofa and vomiting her food but these were still directly attributable to the rather sinister black and white cat (called, we believe, Cuthbert) who had taken to pulling faces at her through the living-room window when he found he couldn't penetrate the defences at the back of the house. The problem was soon resolved relatively easily by securing various objects to the front window sill which made it impossible for Cuthbert to land comfortably and maintain his balance whilst eyeballing. Nothing looks less threatening than a cat about to fall off something backwards.

Time went by and Flossie went from strength to strength. The incidents of urination on the sofa became a thing of the past and Rob felt she was showing him the true cat who had been lying underneath the clingy one all along. He used to keep in touch regularly via emails and one message spoke volumes. *So all in all, we're a much happier household. I'm having those wonderful moments again where I walk into the room or look up and see Flossie and say to myself: look, a cat! And it's in my house!*

As Rob stopped worrying about Flossie so much he relaxed and learnt to enjoy her. She in turn became less distressed by the ever diminishing attentions of Cuthbert and the sofa became an area for sleeping rather than peeing. She continued to gain weight and her coat became glossy as she started to groom herself once more. Excursions outside were no longer such an urgent necessity (Cuthbert soon lost interest) but, if the weather was nice, she could always be found watching Rob as he did a little pruning.

Snuggles – the case of acquired dependency

Dependency can come in many guises and develop in different ways. Snuggles was about ten years old when I met her. She had lived previously with her companion, Bossy, a large elderly black cat, and their relationship had appeared blissfully content. Sadly he had died several months before and his demise had seemed to herald a dramatic change in Snuggles, hence my visit.

Snuggles and Bossy had never been 'in your face' cats; they delighted in each other's company and socialized pleasantly with their owners when the mood took them. They had been perfect pets really, no trouble at all and ideal companions for a busy couple working from home. When Bossy died poor Snuggles seemed to lose the plot. She wandered aimlessly around the house wailing and searching for her misplaced friend. Catherine and Michael, her owners, felt terribly sorry for her and they found themselves comforting her constantly and going about their business with her cradled in their arms like a baby. As soon as they put her down she would start wailing again so they attempted a shift system of attention-providing to reassure their bereaved pet.

A couple of months later they had to go away on business and they arranged for a friend to visit and feed Snuggles whilst they were gone. When they returned they couldn't believe their eyes; their beautiful Snuggles looked moth-eaten and unkempt. She had systematically removed her fur in patches from various locations on her belly, sides and legs. As Michael and Catherine walked round the house they found clumps of fur in little piles as if Snuggles had tugged on her coat and pulled it out in pawfuls. They took her to the vet's the following morning and they did a complicated series of tests to establish a reason for this sudden hair loss. After exhaustive investigation the vet found nothing tangible and referred Snuggles to me as potentially suffering from stress.

When I visited Catherine and Michael it was obvious that Snuggles had started to rule their lives. She was on either his lap or hers throughout our discussions and when she wasn't she sat and licked her coat and pulled chunks out with her teeth. Every time this happened there was a chorus of 'No, Snuggles, darling!' and either Michael or Catherine would scoop her up and rock her gently whilst speaking words of comfort. They reported that sleep was a thing of the past for them both as all they could hear all night was 'lick, lick, pluck, lick, lick, pluck' and it was driving them to distraction. They tried to shut her out but the lick, lick, pluck just continued outside their door accompanied by howls of protest. Every morning they were greeted with piles of hair on the carpet and a cat who had so much loose fur sticking out of her mouth she looked like a cannibal. They decided that allowing her access to the bed was the lesser of two evils. At least she wasn't screaming. Planned holidays were abandoned and their lives were redefined as carers for Snuggles. Unfortunately, despite their best efforts, all the attention they were lavishing upon her failed to stop the constant lick, lick, pluck and incessant whining.

Snuggles was a sweet little creature and her pathetic

appearance and countenance provided the perfect excuse for anyone to pick her up and comfort her. Ironically this was not having the intended effect and Snuggles was becoming totally reliant on reassurance and attention from her owners. Theirs had truly become a dysfunctional relationship, with the added complication that her stress was causing her to pull her fur out. Cats have limited ways to deal with stress; they can't turn to drink or drugs and they can't talk things through with counsellors (which would make my job easier). Instead they have to rely on predictable, safe patterns of behaviour such as eating, grooming and sleeping to fill those times when they need to pacify a worried mind. It isn't a coincidence that the country is full of cats over-eating, over-grooming and sleeping their lives away when faced with difficult situations.

I explained this concept to Catherine and Michael and suggested that a gradual withdrawal of their attention would be a positive step towards her recovery. However, this should never be attempted without first finding an alternative pursuit to distract the cat. Failure to provide other things to do when the owners aren't giving attention can send an already stressed cat into orbit.

Catherine and Michael were blessed with a wonderful garden with a sunny rockery, a pond and shady trees. Snuggles used to go outdoors when Bossy was around but only to follow him and generally bask in his shadow. She had seemed to give up the great outdoors on Bossy's demise and her life now revolved around the Aga, her little wicker bed and her owners. Nothing works better than the smells, sights and sounds of a beautiful garden to revive a depressed cat so I suggested that Snuggles be encouraged to spend more time outside. A new regime began that confined Snuggles to the spacious kitchen at bedtime. Michael and Catherine wouldn't be able to hear the complaints and could (hopefully) avoid the temptation to comfort her in the night. Snuggles was provided with a late supper of her favourite food and her wicker bed was placed next to the Aga. In the morning she would be greeted by her owners and taken outside for her morning constitutional. I suggested that this should initially be an escorted ramble to give her the confidence to soak up the sights, but she would hopefully start to go it alone at some stage.

We were blessed with some good weather over the next two weeks and the arrival of a pair of ducks on the garden pond. Snuggles was captivated by the ducks and would sit crouched at a safe distance just watching them for hours. Catherine put her wicker basket just outside the kitchen door in the sun and Snuggles seemed to be in heaven. Michael and Catherine had been instructed to ignore Snuggles's plucking and screaming. That, as always, was tough but they kept reassuring themselves that giving attention hadn't worked in the past so anything was worth a try. Snuggles continued to approach her owners for the usual attention but their averted eyes and turned backs made her realize all was not right. She tried even harder to get their attention but her swishing tail gave a hint that she was really in two minds about persevering. After all, those ducks were back and the sun was out and the breeze felt good on her bald bits . . .

Several weeks went by and each morning Michael and Catherine were greeted with ever decreasing piles of fur when they opened the door to the kitchen. For the first two weeks they found Snuggles pressed up against the door (I did try to convince them that she had merely responded to their footsteps on the stairs and had not been at the door howling all night) but after that she was found in a variety of different poses and locations in the large room. When they started to find her pressed up against the back door instead, ready to go out, they thought that things were turning the corner. Over-grooming of this kind doesn't disappear overnight and many cats need a little help with the transition to more normal cleaning regimes. Vets often prescribe a type of anti-depressant in these situations but that really wasn't an option for Snuggles as it was felt she was a little old for such aggressive medication. Whilst these drugs are comparatively safe at the appropriate dose a cat's liver isn't really designed to deal with such toxic substances. We knew, therefore, that the old habit of lick, lick, pluck would take some time to disappear.

Eight weeks later Snuggles was transformed. She didn't whinge or whine and she sat outside in her little wicker basket as if she truly owned the place. She had her morning routine of patrolling the boundaries of the walled garden followed by a quick sniff round to see where her duck friends were hanging out. She still popped into the kitchen to see her owners but if they were intent on the morning papers or working on their computers she would turn tail and disappear back outside. She still plucked her coat in a couple of places but Michael and Catherine were delighted to see that her beautiful tabby and white fur was returning in others. They eventually booked a holiday and, despite a little extra fur loss down one front leg, she survived the ordeal of being home alone with a couple of cat-sitters visiting daily.

As cats get older they tend to become more prone to dependency and over-attachment but it isn't inevitable that it will lead to stress-related illness and sleepless nights. Most owners relish the increased attention afforded to them by their elderly felines and nobody suffers. Occasionally other things, such as the death of a cat companion, will tip the balance and cats will develop dependencies (like Snuggles) that don't do anyone any favours. With careful handling and sensitive withdrawal, coupled with alternative activities, a sense of self-reliance can be reinstated and life can go on as before.

Betty, her daughter et al.

Betty and her daughter presented quite a dilemma to me some years ago and I have never forgotten my utter frustration and complete inability to make an ounce of difference. Whilst not exactly an illustration of a dependent cat, it certainly shows how complicated some relationships can be between women and their cats. I'm rather reluctant in a way to describe the details of this particular story since I never really had the answer; guidelines to address similar situations are beyond me. However, we tackled the whole issue with good humour (even if mine was more akin to hysteria) and Betty and Hilary seemed happy enough with the outcome.

The two ladies in question lived together in a small cottage in a quiet village in Sussex. They both initially had full-time jobs and always had a cat in the house. Over the years, and they couldn't say exactly how, they had managed to acquire a total of six feline residents. They had come as strays or from local rescue centres but they all had one thing in common. I found this quite surprising since I can honestly say I had never seen a household with so many cats with similar personalities. They were all scaredy-cats; they were frightened of their own shadow, each other, noises, movement and humans. Just about everything, really, that any cat would encounter in normal domestic life. When I visited Betty and Hilary I caught glimpses, but the cats were mainly nowhere to be seen. I asked them whether the similarity was a coincidence or did they gravitate towards the cowardly, and they didn't really seem to know. They said things like 'we felt sorry for them' and 'nobody else would want them' and 'we thought we could make a difference'.

Sadly, they hadn't quite made the difference they had hoped for. The cats had firmly resisted attempted handling and expressions of love and they had each adopted an area in the house they called their own. Every day they would retreat to these private places or disappear outdoors and only visit or have contact with their owners when it was time to eat. This is where the problem lay and poor Betty and Hilary had got themselves in a bit of a pickle trying to compensate for the lack of affection they could show to their beloved cats. They wanted their charges to feel loved and they decided the best way to achieve this would be to express their devotion through food. So they devised a feeding plan and daily regime that went something like this:

6.00 a.m.   Cook fish for Stripey and Elmo.

6.15 a.m.   Feed the fish to Stripey and Elmo, give rabbit chunks to Monty (in the back bedroom), give tuna in brine to Elsie (under Hilary's bed, other-wise she won't eat), give hypoallergenic biscuits to Sandy and lamb in gravy to TC on top of the kitchen cupboard.

11.00 a.m.   Call all the cats in for elevenses – cooked chicken or tinned ham.

2.00 p.m.   Put lunch down in four different places and hope they all get some whilst calling their names repeatedly.

6.00 p.m.   Cook more fish.

6.15 p.m.   Feed it to Stripey and Elmo, rabbit chunks to Monty, tuna in brine to Elsie, etc.

10.00 p.m.   Fish-flavoured biscuits and prawns for supper (all the cats would usually come in from the garden for such a tasty morsel).

10.15 p.m.   Shut all the cats indoors for the night. Alternatively, stay up until four in the morning trying to get some of them in.

I was scribbling this down as they spoke, thinking all the while that this seemed to be an impossible regime and that one week of it would have sent me mad. I was not surprised to hear that poor Betty had given up her job six months earlier because she just didn't have time to work. She had also become increasingly reluctant to go outside or carry out any errands that required leaving the house for any length of time since she was concerned the cats would panic if she wasn't around. She even did most of her cleaning with a dustpan and brush since she was concerned that the vacuum cleaner would distress them.

Hilary had managed to keep a degree of perspective and she constantly scolded her mother for her obsessive behaviour. This just created friction between mother and daughter and made matters worse. Betty knew it was wrong, but there didn't seem to be any alternative now that she had started living her life that way. After all, some of the cats were coming to her now and nagging her for food. Surely that meant that she was loved and needed?

I shall never forget that visit to Betty and Hilary. I spent four hours there and we talked and talked. We looked at options and consequences and eventually it was unanimously agreed that none of the cats would suffer if we changed the regime and gave Betty back a little of her life. Betty sat forward in her seat and nodded with great enthusiasm as I detailed a new feeding regime and way of life for her and her cats. Gone were the days when she would follow them round, look at them and speak to them all the time. Gone were the days when she stayed up all night to make sure they came in; it had never been an effective ploy anyway because they still came in when they wanted to and not before. We were also going to radically change the hugely expensive and wasteful feeding regime to well-balanced nutritional meals that would suit all palates. I felt quite proud of myself when I left that house because I was convinced that four hours of persuasion and coercion had shown Betty the light and things would be different from then on. Fat chance!

I had a call from Hilary several days later. Nothing had changed except that Betty had become even more stressed because she couldn't adhere to the new regime. She still stayed up all night, she still fed fish and tuna under the bed and she still swept her floors rather than use a noisy cleaner. I asked Hilary to put Betty on the phone; I wanted to hear her side of the story and why she thought she was failing so dismally. It was quite simple, really: she couldn't resist the cats. To deprive them of their food and their routines would be cruel. She was the one who had to change and she would just have to get used to the sleep deprivation, the loss of earnings and the constant struggle from one meal to the next. Logic had clearly gone up in smoke but I found myself almost understanding where she was coming from. These cats were her life now and their per-ceived feelings and wishes actually outweighed her own. She couldn't possibly attempt to change anything for her own sake since that would undoubtedly have been totally selfish. What a dilemma. I tried very hard over the telephone to emphasize that the changes needed to be made for the cats' benefit but she wasn't convinced. I even made her a plastic-coated poster to put up in the kitchen with all the rules of the new regime but it failed to impress.

Some weeks later we had reached a stalemate. Betty was very unhappy as she couldn't follow the programme at all. Hilary was unhappy because Betty couldn't follow the programme and there were constant arguments. I returned to their house, determined to have a last go at improving things for everyone. I suppose I succeeded on one level; both Hilary and Betty fully accepted I was right. However, Betty was suffering from emotional inertia. She couldn't change just in case the alterations were disapproved of by the cats. She was helpless.

There are occasions when I just have to walk away. This really had become Betty's problem and my field of expertise is with the cats not the owners. I knew the cats would benefit from my suggestions but I was powerless to help. I was honest with Betty and explained my frustration. I wanted to make her life and that of her cats better. I wanted to make a difference, but I couldn't. I often feel that that particular case taught me as much about myself and my motivation for doing this job as it did about Betty!

Chunky – dependency works both ways

I once had a client called Terri; I remember her with some affection because she was such a nice person. I also remember her because she illustrated so well how complicated (and self-destructive) love for a cat can be. Many times when I have lost one of my wonderful cats I have sobbed 'I'm never having cats again; it's too painful when they die!' and I know I'm not the only cat lover to have said that. A great deal of the emotion we feel for these creatures is painful and occasionally, as Terri found, the pleasure of ownership becomes a distant memory but the love remains with a vengeance.

Terri called me in tears to ask if I could help her dear old Chunky. It was hard to accurately ascertain over the telephone what was grieving her about her fourteen-year-old cat; she talked of depression, anxiety, not adjusting to his new home, illness . . . I spoke to her veterinary surgeon, a personal friend of mine, and it was agreed that I would visit Terri to see what could be done to make Chunky happier.

Terri and her husband, Joe, lived in a newly built house that they had moved into only two months prior to my visit. They were surrounded by JCB diggers, noise and mud and their pristine home sat with three or four other occupied properties on a massive building site. I was shown into her lovely new sitting room and I sat down next to the curled-up figure of a little black and white cat (not so chunky now), breathing deeply and fast asleep. Terri sat on the other side of him on the sofa and, as she fiddled, caressed and poked him, she told me his story.

Chunky had lived with Terri from a tiny kitten. He had been every young girl's ideal pet, a real tomcat outdoors and a gentle creature full of affection for his young owner indoors after a busy day's hunting in the fields surrounding her family home. Chunky was with Terri when she met Joe and, when they decided to marry, he moved with them to their first new home. He accepted Joe and even started to show him great affection once he had registered his initial protest through cool in-difference. Life carried on and all three were perfectly happy going about their normal day-to-day business for the next ten years. Sadly, since then, things had not been so good for Terri; she had been made redundant and found it difficult to get another job, there had been money worries, her father had become seriously ill, her best friend had died and Chunky had had a series of worrying illnesses. He had developed a cancerous growth on his face (that had subsequently been removed) and then suffered a mysterious problem with bald patches that had virtually appeared overnight. Terri had found it all too much and, combined with the recent house move, she had become seriously depressed and anxious and was now on anti-depressants in order to cope.

Chunky had not adjusted well to the move. He seemed to hate all the noise and a young cat next door insisted on sitting on the fence and staring through the patio doors at him. He had lost his appetite and suffered from intermittent explosive diarrhoea. The vet had suggested he might be suffering from inflammatory bowel disease and had prescribed an easily digestible prescription diet. Chunky hated the new food; Terri was panicking and Chunky just looked downright depressed. He was no longer the sleek, muscle-bound hunter of old. He didn't want to go outdoors any more and, when he wasn't emitting diarrhoea, he just slept for hours on end. He looked frail and Terri was petrified that she was going to lose him.

Terri and Chunky had become very close over the years. He had always spent a lot of his time outdoors but every moment spent inside was devoted to Terri. She loved him with a passion and focused totally on him. He loved the attention and the relationship was described by Terri as being 'completely tuned in to one another'. Chunky would never leave her side when she was sad or ill. He seemed to understand those moments when she needed him most.

Terri had very eloquently described how she felt about her cat. She also fully understood that she was at a low ebb and everything seemed worrying and out of control. There are many occasions in my work when the owners' emotional state has an enormous impact on their cats. It is a constant challenge to understand the implications of this and work to address it whilst ensuring that the owner doesn't feel that I am trying to help them emotionally too. I am not a psychologist and there are many times when I have said to my clients, 'I wish I could help but I'm not qualified; you should see someone.' However, I have to understand what motivates the client because, as in this case, their behaviour can be at the very least influential, and at the worst the primary cause of the cat's problem.

I spent the next half an hour explaining to Terri, as gently as possible, what the past few years had been like from Chunky's perspective. He had suffered from a tumour and had undergone several stressful visits to the veterinary practice culminating in uncomfortable surgery. His owner had changed her behaviour dramatically and been obviously persistently worried by the events in her personal life. Her anxiety would have been viewed by Chunky as a response to danger so he would have felt an element of her distress. As time progressed he was getting older and therefore less secure and Terri's behaviour (and the obvious changes in the household routines that would have been evident) would have heightened that insecurity. This may have been the motivation for his overgrooming. A house move followed and he found himself living on a noisy building site in a completely new territory. As an old insecure cat with an insecure and nervous owner, would he really have felt robust enough to take on the challenge of exploring?

There was also another twist to the tale that Terri hadn't mentioned but I had observed throughout our discussions. She just couldn't leave him alone. She was poking him and fiddling with him and waking him up from his restful sleep. She admitted that, when he went off his food, she was frantic and would spend hours chasing round after him with various bowls of tempting food. She even recalled crying and beseeching him to eat something whilst trying to thrust a prawn into his face. Trust me, this is not the most effective way to promote a healthy appetite. It almost always has the opposite effect and can give cats serious psychological hang-ups about food and eating. I soon discovered that many of Chunky's bouts of diarrhoea were more than likely to have been caused by eating a huge variety of rich foods provided by an anxious owner. It is certainly true that stress can cause intestinal disturbances but Terri's over-zealous attempts to feed were probably making things worse. Both Terri and Chunky were locked into a cycle of stress, anxiety and depression. Something had to change and undoubtedly that something was Terri.

She was a smart lady and as I discussed the position with her it was clear that she suddenly realized the implications of her actions. I always try to be amusing in my consultations no matter how distressing the facts of the case may be. This doesn't mean I appear heartless; I make sure the owner understands why I joke on occasions. Terri, like practically all my clients, had a keen sense of humour and after shedding many tears during our meeting was soon laughing at the image of her crawling round after Chunky, trying to push food into a cat who clearly thought she had gone mad.

We devised a plan for the future. Chunky's bowel had obviously become sensitive so it was agreed that she would feed the prescribed diet exclusively. A small bowl of slightly warmed food would be placed in Chunky's normal feeding area and Terri would walk away. She would not look at him or encourage him, and if he hadn't eaten it within half an hour the food would be removed and another helping would be put down a few hours later. Chunky wasn't active at all so it was entirely likely that his appetite would be smaller than usual and non-existent some days. Terri also agreed that she would stop touching Chunky all the time and waking him up. Older cats normally sleep for 75 per cent of the day and it's never pleasant to be woken from a deep sleep.

During the consultation I had played with Chunky using a piece of string. He thoroughly enjoyed it and even went outside shortly afterwards for the first time in weeks. Sometimes it pays to stop treating old cats like invalids! Terri was certainly impressed by his sudden youthful response and she promised to play with him regularly rather than hold his paw and gaze dolefully into his eyes. She vowed to stop all over-concerned behaviour around him and I agreed that it would be more beneficial to voice any worries to me over the telephone than to let Chunky see her anxiety. I couldn't take away Terri's depression or her stress after everything that had happened recently in her life but I could hopefully help her to understand the potential impact on Chunky. I left that afternoon full of hope that things would soon change for the better.

Three days later I had the first phone call from her to say that she had noticed an incredible improvement. Chunky seemed much happier and he had started to eat the prescription food; not much, but enough to reassure her that he wouldn't starve to death. He was spending more time sitting in the garden and even Joe had noticed that Chunky was more alert and like his old self. We had taken away the stressful impact of Terri's insistent behaviour, and when she relaxed, Chunky relaxed too. To his brain, the crisis she was expressing was obviously over. I cannot say that Terri was never con-cerned about Chunky's health again or that she didn't occasionally wake him up to squeeze him or hold his paw. It did, however, become a less tense relationship for the rest of Chunky's days. He died two years later, peacefully at home, with Terri at his side.

BF – the obsessed cat

It is interesting to see that the last two cases have illustrated the dependent element of a human/cat relationship as very much the owner's problem. Dependent cats are often created by a dependent human but every now and then, in a cat behaviour counsellor's lifetime, we get to see a truly bizarre case that illustrates how complicated the domestic cat can be. I was contacted by a lady in Scotland, Jane, who worked for one of the large animal rescue charities. She wanted support with a distressing case and asked if I would be willing to help her via the telephone and relevant videos. I agreed to assist if I could and asked her to tell me the story of BF. He had arrived in the charity's cattery as a ten-week-old kitten and at the age of five months he was transferred into a foster home. He remained there with a number of other young cats for four months and during this time he went missing. He had left the foster home as an affectionate and loving kitten but he returned with a problem. He started to defecate randomly in front of the foster carers on carpets or hard floors; it didn't seem to matter. The common denominator was that he emptied his bowel as near to the humans as possible. They found this intolerable after a time and returned him to Jane's cattery. Jane already had several cats of her own and didn't feel she could cope with another full time in her house. She had a dilemma, though, because the alternative was to return BF to an outdoor pen and chalet. She compromised by allowing him restricted access to her home during the day for a couple of hours, access to the garden and the pen at night.

He settled well, and seemed to be perfectly happy with her other cats, but there was something very strange about BF. He wouldn't keep still; he latched on to Jane immediately and didn't want to leave her side for a second. His toilet habits were not the best. He always urinated in the various litter trays provided or in appropriate areas of Jane's garden, but he defecated wherever he felt like it, preferably on or near Jane's feet. If he was away from her he would content himself with eliminating right in the middle of his pen or on the lawn. It's really nice when cats seem to want our company twenty-four hours a day but it soon loses its appeal when you cannot sit down or stand for any length of time without a cat climbing up your legs and trying to put its head in your mouth. That was BF's other party piece. Whenever he saw Jane he would become so excited that he would start to hyperventilate (breathing rapidly through his mouth). He would then climb up her body and attempt to push his head into her mouth. This cat didn't sleep since his whole purpose in life seemed to be to get to Jane. Once there, his response was to defecate and get thoroughly over-excited.

Jane sent me a video and I studied it in detail. I have to admit I found it quite distressing. The video showed BF pacing backwards and forwards in his pen, crawling up Jane and defecating on a shelf when he saw her. Jane's veterinary surgeon had been puzzled by his behaviour and prescribed a tricyclic anti-depressant to try to calm him. The drug he chose had once been used to treat humans with obsessive-compulsive disorder. BF was given a relatively high dose but rather than make him calm or even a little dozy it seemed to have the opposite effect. I was completely perplexed. I contacted colleagues in the Association of Pet Behaviour Counsellors and we discussed all sorts of possibilities. Some suggested it was a rather dog-like bonding disorder, a mixture of frustration and fearful insecurity. Others thought it might be an unusual attention-seeking behaviour that had been inadvertently reinforced by Jane and the previous owners. I even remember some talk of ADHD (attention deficit hyperactivity disorder) in cats.

We tried increased stimulation, challenging feeding regimes, the introduction of other carers and various other ideas to focus him elsewhere. Robin Walker, my wonderful colleague and friend and a real expert on such things, suggested that the paradoxical effect of the anti-depressant could have been due to a deficiency of a certain chemical in BF's brain called serotonin (a mood-stabilizing hormone). He gave advice on a home-made diet to provide nutrients that converted to serotonin but we were just too late. I received a letter from Jane saying: *BF put to sleep 9.20 a.m. today. A very sad day for all who knew him. I will miss him very much. Thanks for all you have done.* Several years later I still don't understand what happened to BF to make him behave in this way. I am still searching for the answers.

Damson and Cherry and the delights of ylang-ylang soap

I see a lot of undesirable attention-seeking behaviour, but there is little that competes with this case. Damson and Cherry were two delightful (if somewhat 'in your face') lilac Burmese sisters. They lived with their stylish and equally delightful owner called Arabella. I visited them because the two cats were causing havoc in the home and Arabella felt powerless to control their wilful behaviour. Over the telephone I had heard stories of launched attacks and bizarre eating habits including recent surgery to remove a foreign body from Damson's intestines. Apparently she had been shut into the bedroom one day and, in sheer frustration, had eaten the carpet. I was somewhat apprehensive when I arrived at the apartment.

I was greeted enthusiastically by Arabella and directed into one of the most exquisite rooms I have ever seen. It was a fairy-tale land of cream, gold and white with embroidered cushions, fur throws, thick carpet and huge lumps of quartz crystal everywhere. The lighting was soft and the whole impression was one of tranquillity and calm until the two Burmese skidded into the room. My first impression when I saw them was 'Gosh, what skinny Burmese!' They were five years old when we met so there was no question they were juveniles waiting to fill out. Whilst attractive, they certainly looked as if they needed a good meal. As I sat taking notes and listening to Arabella's story I watched in fascination as Damson and Cherry worked as a team around the room, intent on achieving centre stage and their owner's full attention. Damson jumped on a shelf and pushed a crystal candlestick slowly and purposefully towards the edge. As Arabella leapt to the aid of the fragile ornament it was Cherry's turn to take a silk cushion in her mouth and chew it, staring directly at her owner. Arabella turned quickly, still talking, and whisked the cushion away before too much damage had been done. Every movement and response to their continuous taunts was swift and obviously well rehearsed; Arabella had definitely done this before.

It's quite wrong of me to use such subjective language when talking about cats but it was impossible to see any of their behaviour as anything but a well-planned attention-seeking game. Their every destructive action was being met by Arabella's immediate response, the most fascinating element being the way they seemed to take it in turns to display each new and devious plot to keep their owner on the go.

Arabella told me that she had acquired them as kittens to keep her company during her long working days at home. She was a designer and she worked in a small studio attached to the living room. She bought two, thinking they would be company for each other, but she had had no idea they would eventually work as a team to send her completely mad. Her biggest worry was the 'kitchen fiasco' as she referred to it; she suggested that I sit down in the comfort of the living room and witness the carnage as she went to make some coffee. As she got up to walk in that direction both Burmese rushed in front of her and swiftly jumped to the top of the kitchen cabinets, one on either side of the door. She entered the room (slightly hunched and obviously bracing herself for something) and both cats leapt towards her. Damson bounced off her left shoulder and landed on the work surface. Cherry clutched on to her back and hair and remained there as she tried to switch the kettle on. The whole thing looked hideously uncomfortable and very stressful as every cupboard that was opened was immediately filled by two lilac cats. Arabella explained that they raided the bin and the cupboards constantly and had even tried a four-pawed attempt to open the fridge. Cooking for herself was now impossible unless she nipped into the kitchen when they weren't looking and shut the door just long enough to avoid them eating the carpet on the other side. How could she live like this?

I asked Arabella about their unusual eating habits (behaviour referred to as 'pica') and she listed a whole catalogue of tasty treats including fabric, plastic, cardboard and their absolute favourite, ylang-ylang soap. When I asked what more conventional food they ate I wasn't surprised to hear the answer. She divided half a tin of Whiskas between the two cats; this she gave to them in four small meals throughout the day. Herself a strict vegetarian, she also gave them rice, potatoes, vegetables and fruit in small quantities. She was extremely anxious about their becoming overweight so she was very precise in the amounts she fed. The only thing she couldn't control was their consumption of her furniture and possessions.

We chatted for a while longer and I commented how svelte Damson and Cherry were (a euphemism in my book for 'far too thin'). Her reply alarmed me. She thanked me for the compliment, and said, 'I really do believe you can never be too rich or too thin and that goes for my cats too!'

There is a tremendous temptation for some people to inflict their particular views, habits and lifestyle choices on their pets. I suppose I should have been grateful that Arabella hadn't imposed her strict vegetarianism on her cats; they would of course be dead now if she had – meat protein is essential for their survival. She was, however, imposing her views on weight on them and this was leaving the poor things permanently starving. This is the only case I have ever seen where the consumption of non-nutritional substances was actually about hunger.

I had to be careful since I didn't want to contradict Arabella or appear to judge her for what she was doing. After all, she loved these cats and wanted desperately to do the right thing. I explained to her that Damson and Cherry were actually underweight and this left them with a huge appetite and an owner they saw as the only source of proper food. Their lives had therefore started to focus round Arabella and gaining her attention at all times, especially when she was in the room that housed all the edible stuff. We needed to feed the cats more and take away the perception of Arabella as the provider. Increasing their dietary intake would have to be done extremely gradually since too much too soon would probably only result in regurgitation or vomiting. I calculated an accurate daily increase of the cat food and an introduction of a cat biscuit to enable Arabella to abandon the vegetable and carbohydrate titbits. I explained to Arabella that my main aim was to get both the cats on dry complete cat food only. This would enable her to feed throughout the day by secreting the biscuits in various places. The cats (let's face it – they were bright) would search round the apartment and find all the food without Arabella's being involved. For the period of the programme we put away cushions, soap, cardboard and all things seen as 'edible' by Damson and Cherry. We introduced more cat toys, water fountains, scratching posts and paraphernalia to increase their general level of entertainment. I felt it was also important to have a few more house rules; Arabella had really lost control of her life. I asked her to ignore their attention-seeking with clear signals – no speaking and no eye or physical contact. Any response, even shouting, would be seen by the cats as a victory. The kitchen door was shut when Arabella was in it and her studio door was shut when she was working. Fixing the handles so that they worked only when they were pulled upwards solved the dilemma of both cats' being able to open doors by swinging on the handles. At last Arabella felt she had the chance to get one step ahead of the dastardly duo!

I received a phone call a couple of weeks later from Arabella and the news was encouraging. She had followed the gradual increase in food to the letter and the cats were now receiving the appropriate daily allowance of complete cat biscuits. Damson and Cherry were highly delighted to find these pellets of food hidden in small empty plant pots in various parts of their home and they spent hours running from one room to the next to see what treasures they could discover. Arabella reported that they seemed calmer and less active; she couldn't remember the last time she had seen them sleeping for long periods during the day. I cautioned her about getting complacent. Her strategy of ignoring their attention-seeking behaviour was working at this early stage but cats like Damson and Cherry have a habit of regrouping and coming back with a blistering counter-attack that is difficult to overlook. She had to maintain her resolve and continue to ignore their unreasonable demands.

As predicted, the counter-attack came as Damson started to stand on the back of the sofa or the mantelpiece and bang the paintings on the wall with her paw. This caused them to rock precariously and, sure enough, Arabella dashed to their rescue, thinking of injured cats and damaged artwork. Immediately, she could have kicked herself, but her instincts had taken over. She knew what had to be done and all pictures that were remotely accessible to either cat were removed and placed with everything else in the now bulging-at-the-seams cupboard.

As the weeks went by the cats became a little bored with the flower pots so Arabella and I agreed we needed the versatility of cardboard to make the acquisition of their biscuits even more challenging. I love building pyramids from toilet roll tubes (so that cats can use their paws to pull out individual biscuits) but had resisted the temptation in this case, given the cats' previous eating habits. However, now was the time to put their progress to the test and Arabella set out cardboard boxes, loo-roll pyramids and paper bags to make things a little tougher. Miraculously the cardboard remained intact – well, almost – and we felt a little chewing was a small price to pay and a perfectly normal response to material of this kind.

Damson and Cherry never became fat cats. Any vet would have been proud of their optimum weight and healthy physique. Arabella continued to have the occasional problem with them. It was so tempting for her to let her guard down and allow them to sit in the kitchen while she cooked, or distract her from her work. As soon as she did so they started bullying her again and she realized that she would never be able to be anything but a strict disciplinarian. The phrase 'give them an inch and they'll take a mile' could have been coined with these two characters in mind.

❉   ❉   ❉

Whether your cat's dependency is manifesting itself in attention-seeking, helplessness, manipulation or anxiety there is one essential thing to remember: dependencies are not in the best interests of either party. Many owners call me for advice because their cats are keeping them up at night, vocalizing excessively or demanding food, and every one without exception feels guilty if they ignore their furry friend. Many of these cats live exclusively indoors and the owners believe that they have to give in to their every whim to keep them happy. Often the reverse is true. Dependencies don't make the cats happy at all. I have had my own personal battle with my lovely little Devon Rex, Mangus. She has tried every trick in the book with me and I will admit I have succumbed during moments of weakness. I am then rewarded with the most insistent and ridiculous behaviour for about a week until she eventually goes back to normal. I increase the activities provided for her in my flat and decrease my availability. The result is always a more content Mangus so I can honestly say I know what owners are going through when they live with a dependent cat – and I know what gets results!

Tackling dependency by changing the relationship

Dependency is a downward spiral; for example, the more you reassure your cat the more helpless he or she will become. Whilst it's great to feel loved it's important to understand that you can only maintain this relationship if you are there for your cat twenty-four hours a day. If you dare to sleep or go shopping you may have a problem. Dysfunctional dependencies can be avoided by following these suggestions:

- Do a quick 'activity budget' on your cat's typical day. If it only includes sleeping and following you around like a bad smell then you may have a problem!
- Encourage your cat to be a cat as much as possible. If he or she has access to a garden then make sure it is a safe and attractive environment. The more time your cat spends doing cat things the less likely he or she will be to need your constant attention.
- If you live on a busy road it may be possible to build an out-side enclosure or secure your garden to keep your cat safe.
- Bullying from other cats can be a problem too and it can prevent insecure types from exploring. Securing your garden will keep them out.
- If you are busy, relaxing or otherwise occupied it is perfectly acceptable to deny your cat attention. This will not make them love you less; it may actually make you more attractive!
- Consider feeding your cat 'ad lib' with a dry complete cat food. This will encourage grazing little and often (a very

natural way for a cat to take in food) and take away the emphasis on you as the sole provider of sustenance.

- Feel free to visit friends, work for a living or go on holiday. You are perfectly entitled to a life too and your cat will be delighted to see you when you return rather than pining away to nothing when you leave. Start as you mean to go on; even servants get time off.

- It isn't essential to share your bed with your cat. They often cope extremely well if they are given a quiet, warm area to snooze the night away, without your snoring and constant thrashing about. This can teach them an important lesson: that life can be good without you.

- Some cats benefit from four-legged companions and this can take the heat off you. Dogs and cats can work well (see Chapter 5) and even other cats can be a blessing for those likely to form close attachments.

- If you feel your cat is exhibiting problem behaviour resulting from a dependency, call in an expert with a referral from your vet. Sometimes we are all just too close to the relationship to change it for the better without professional help.

CHAPTER 9

Why Do We Love Cats So Much?

MY JOB IS THE SORT OF CAREER THAT REQUIRES ALL KINDS OF objective analysis from time to time. In my darker moments I have even asked 'What's in it for the cat?' and questioned the whole concept of pet ownership. Is it really as good for them as it is for us? Luckily, I have come to the conclusion (all things being equal) that the relationship between human and cat is positive for both parties and here to stay. I think this is a fascinating subject and worthy of further exploration. In order to get the best out of the relationship for both parties we have to at least attempt to understand our cats better. This is not about judging ourselves (I include myself in every comment and theory I have); it's far more constructive than that. I just want to know why we love them so much!

In my quest for a better understanding of the human/cat relationship I felt it necessary to start from a more familiar viewpoint: human/human relationships. There are literally thousands of self-help books available that offer advice on and analysis of every conceivable relationship we may possibly encounter during a lifetime. As far as I can tell (and I've read many of them) they mostly fall into the following categories:

1 How to be a good parent and not mess up your children.
2 How to survive childhood (if your parents didn't read Book 1).
3 How to get the best out of work relationships to guarantee promotion.
4 How to attract a possible partner and start a relationship.
5 How to make the most of your relationship and ensure it lasts.
6 How to understand your partner who apparently comes from another planet.
7 How to spot the tell-tale signs if your partner is having an affair.
8 How to avoid displaying the tell-tale signs if *you* are having an affair.
9 How to survive a relationship break-up after you read Book 7 and he *didn't* read Book 8.

This is not an exhaustive list, but you get the picture that this is a very overworked genre. I read five or six books on this topic in quick succession and my main concern was that they encourage over-analysis and rather too much soul searching. I can't help feeling that you will find a problem if you look hard enough. My other suspicion is that I am inadvertently adding to the list by writing a book specifically about our relationships with our cats. Maybe they don't merit analysis? Maybe delving too deeply will merely open a Pandora's box of issues we would rather not address? If, however, it produces one tiny piece of enlightenment that enriches our cats' lives it has to be worth it. These relationships must *never* be about our specific needs alone and maybe appreciating those needs honestly will enable us to accept that cats have needs too and they are probably not the same as ours.

The female/feline attraction

In this chapter I want to look first at the extraordinary nature of the female/feline attraction. I am still not entirely satisfied that describing cats as feminine and sensual is enough to explain the obsession we women have with them. There has been a great deal written over the years about why women seem to gravitate towards cats and become so besotted with them. It is quite clear that, given the history of the cat's domestication, this is not a modern-day phenomenon. Whilst we may make more extreme emotional demands on our cats these days it seems that they have been demigods in the eyes of humans for many thousands of years. We may not bow in front of them any more or worship them in the religious sense, but we do rather surround ourselves with symbols and effigies (how many cat ornaments have you got?). We also love them to distraction and give them just about anything their hearts desire. Most of us do fall apart when we lose them and show immense grief, falling short only when it comes to shaving our eyebrows off as the Egyptians did. Have things really changed all that much?

There is no doubt that women have incredibly complex emotional needs. We turn to our partners, children, friends and family to fulfil those needs but, sometimes, it just isn't enough. Many women cat lovers I have spoken to over the years talk about their human relationships. Their stories are full of perceptions of disappointment and lack of loyalty; somehow humans never quite get it right. Men are often described as distant and uncommunicative, leaving a woman's emotional needs largely unfulfilled. Then, just when we need them most, along come the nation's cats: small humans, we think, in zip-up furry coats. We may deny we see them like that, but on some level, it is true. We stare longingly at them, we talk to them constantly, we touch them, we caress them and we kiss them. If your cat was a small child in a zip-up furry coat it is possible that he or she might flourish under such conditions of intense love and adoration, but I must admit I'm not convinced. Children surely would be smothered by a love as intensely demonstrated as that? And if you tried to love a partner in the same way as you love your cat, he or she would definitely not find it so attractive: you would look intensely needy. Cats cannot question our unreasonable demands for attention and affection; they can either put up or shut up. They may respond by becoming dependent and needy themselves or capitalize on our incredible compliance and run rings around us. Whatever they choose to do in response to our intense devotion it will never be disloyal and they will never betray us. The beauty of the ambiguity of their communication is that they 'say' whatever we want them to say. They can act their part in any complicated emotional scenario and be word-perfect because we give them the lines. No matter what we need from a relationship at any given time, we have it right there in a curled-up furry ball at the bottom of our bed. I am convinced that a cat provides the sort of relationship that we need, but cannot have with our children, friends or partners.

Do women and cats have something in common?

In defence of those who believe I am merely over-complicating the situation, I should say that it is entirely possible we just like cats because they are beautiful, entertaining, soft and cute. An alternative theory could even be that the relationship between cat and woman works so well because we can relate to so many of their unique traits. Whilst promoting *Cat Detective*, my previous book, I was interviewed by a number of radio presenters for regional BBC stations. One I remember with some interest. I won't mention names but he started the interview by saying, perfectly politely, that he didn't like cats because they were so like women. My immediate response was to ask what he was actually telling me: did he dislike women (and cats merely reminded him of them) or were cats the real enemy and women appeared feline and therefore unpleasant? He said that cats were manipulative, devious and confusing, thus mirroring the worst traits of the average woman. Are cats like women? Do we gravitate towards them because we feel empathy? I would like to think cats *are* like women, because they are graceful and tactile; most of us would love to believe we are elegant and almost all of us are touchy-feely. However, cats are indeed great exponents of psychological warfare; maybe this is the equivalent of the games some women play to get their own way. Women often resort to verbal manipulation and gestures of appeasement and other passive techniques but this is where the similarity ends. Cats prefer not to resort to violence because they themselves are too dangerous; women prefer not to because they are not physically dangerous enough. Correct me if I'm wrong; this does look like a similar survival strategy but I don't think it means we are one and the same.

Are cats just bad boys?

Just to put the cat amongst the pigeons, I have my own personal theory. I have offered it up for general consumption during many late-night discussions with various people, both cat lovers and (dare I say it) cat non-lovers. Most if not all have nodded sagely whilst saying it's an interesting way of looking at the root of the cat's appeal to women. Very few have flatly refuted it as rubbish; admittedly one or two have patted me gently on the head and filled up my wine glass but I remain undeterred. I'll discuss it with you and leave you to reach your own conclusions. I dearly want to deny that this is a plausible theory on *any* level but I just can't.

There is a book called *He's just not that into you: the no-excuses truth to understanding guys*. It gives advice to women who hang on the every word of men who don't return their calls, don't turn up and generally treat them badly. As far as I can remember it was a bestseller and prompted a great deal of discussion in newspapers and women's magazines. There is also a saying 'Treat them mean, keep them keen', implying that the best way to win fair maiden is to feign complete disinterest. Neither the book nor the saying would exist if the phenomenon of women loving 'bad boys' wasn't real and alive in the twenty-first century. I find it quite appalling that women can be attracted to dismissive people and it's hard to rationalize the motivation. I would like to think that most of us would see the obvious error in falling for such a man since it would inevitably end in tears or frustration at the very least. However, we still do it, even though we are now fortunate enough to live in a society where we are perfectly capable, both financially and practically, of caring for ourselves. This made me question whether or not this attraction was desirable from an evolutionary perspective. There has to be an innate attraction to virile men with high testosterone levels and a high sex drive. Such men represent healthy specimens who would be excellent providers and defenders, thereby increasing the odds of the offspring's survival. The more 'male' an individual is (according to all the current gender studies) the more likely they are to be competitive, aggressive, non-communicative and seriously not in tune with the desires of women to be loved and cosseted. These men are the sort of guys who don't praise you, never give a word of encouragement and certainly don't know the meaning of the word compliment. However, if they happen by some miracle to say 'nice dress' we are overwhelmed with gratitude and continue with our attempts to solicit the next loving gesture.

The whole 'treat 'em mean, keep 'em keen' philosophy represents a type of reward referred to in learning theory as partial reinforcement. If behaviour is reinforced occasionally, but certainly not always, it becomes more strongly learnt. For example, the nature of the gambler is such that they thrive on partial reinforcement. They keep going because, every now and then, they are rewarded big time. I don't think it's that great a leap to suggest that women are, to some extent, emotional gamblers – hooked on achieving the odd gesture or sentiment expressed by an otherwise dour individual with much more important things on his mind. We twenty-first century women have a veneer of sophistication that allows us to override this primitive urge but, if we are honest with ourselves, are we not addicted on some level to dismissive and aloof men?

This is where I make another theoretical leap to the nature of the woman/cat relationship. Are not cats capable of being dismissive and aloof? If you look at the results of the relationship survey in the next chapter, you will see that 50 per cent of owners had been ignored by their dismissive cats and 38 per cent, responding to a different set of questions, referred to their cats as 'aloof' on occasion. How many times do owners use the sentence 'He/she is very loving but very much on his/her own terms'? Yet still we pursue them in this feline version of an addictive partial reinforcement programme. I accept that not all cats are made the same and neither are all women; I just keep thinking there is something in this. I have found myself recently being very self-aware when I am round Mangus and I am guilty of the most fickle behaviour sometimes. She has moments of solitude when she wants to be alone and independent and I call and call to get her into the bedroom with me at night to no avail. I go looking for her just to give her a cuddle and feel delighted when she brushes past only to become frustrated when she walks casually away. However, when she is in a 'clingy/in your face' mood she drives me nuts and I can't wait to get into my bedroom to shut the door for a bit of peace from her neediness. Is it just me who sees the parallels between this sort of behaviour and a typical male/female courtship? I'm not saying all female owners behave in this way towards their cats; I just feel that to say women like them because they show unconditional love is a bit simplistic and not really the whole picture.

Men love cats too!

I do have a tendency to focus completely, when discussing this topic, on women. This is totally appropriate since most of my clients are women, most of the people who read my books are women and 96 per cent of all the helpful cat owners who completed the relationship survey discussed in the next chapter were women. However, every now and then, I come into contact with the other 4 per cent. Whilst loving their cats, in my experience, seems to come quite naturally to gay men, every now and again I am privileged enough to be there when heterosexual men open up about their love for their feline companions. I always listen intently because you never know when you are going to receive the piece of information that represents the missing bit of the puzzle.

I have been sent many letters over the years and occasionally I receive them from men. Those that show the true nature of the human/cat relationship best are those written when the cat dies. This particular gentleman was indeed speaking about the loss of his cat. He wrote: *There is an aching void here, quite impossible to describe. Since his friend Hughie cat left us some five years ago, Lenny and I have been very dependent on each other. So much love and understanding. He was eighteen years old and understood my pattern of life in great detail – gentle, loving, constant and so faithful. I miss him enormously and nothing can fill his place in my life. And I will always think of him and miss him terribly – my dear dead lovely Lenny. Bless you, my friend.* I could almost feel the pain when I read this and it was quite clear that Lenny had been his dear companion, particularly since the death of the other member of the household, Hughie cat. Here was a constant in this man's life and it was gone and he was obviously struggling to come to terms with life alone.

I was in my office one day writing this book when I received a phone call from a gentleman who had lost his cat about a year previously. He was obviously an extraordinarily intelligent and eloquent man, a senior lecturer at a university, but he wanted answers about the last few moments of his cat's life. We spoke for some time about the subject but mainly we focused on a more philosophical approach to the subject of loving and losing a pet. He asked me about the nature of the cat's mind and its sentience. I could discuss some of my own thoughts and feelings on the subject but there was definitely a point beyond which I couldn't go because I just didn't have the answers. He told me that he had kept a notebook and he wanted me to read it. I asked his permission to reproduce some of it here because I think it is extremely relevant. I have, however, changed the name of his cat and omitted to mention his to respect his privacy.

He wrote:

I have kept a notebook since my cat was put to sleep. The book is now filled and though I have another one of the same size I set out to complete my reconciliation with the facts by the time I reached the end of this one. I have not used the other one and I don't think I have anything more to say that would be useful to me.

I kept the diary because I did not think I could talk to anyone about what happened. Because there were medical details I wanted to understand there was no point in talking to anyone who did not know anything about them. In addition there were questions about Harry's own physical experience and mental life that I could never discuss with another person who had not arrived at the same understanding as me. People, even vets, might be sympathetic; but I did not need sympathy. I needed knowledge.

If I had not expressed or articulated my thoughts and feelings about the death of my cat I would still be going around in circles or getting sunk in some kind of emotional swamp. I know some people 'steel' themselves and 'not talk about it'. But these are just defences against hurt. Unless this pain is properly explored there can be no understanding and no release. Defences against emotional pain erect an artificial wall between emotion and thought and prevent understanding. Being 'macho' about these things is just so much stupidity. I suspect those who adopt this attitude (it can hardly be called thought) towards animals have not allowed themselves time to think what they are doing. Perhaps they have been swept up in that community of people with 'practical common sense' whose commercial values crowd out less practical forms of thought. This includes assumptions about 'animals' that places them in some order of worth rather than the developing complexity of evolution.

If I was to understand what happened to Harry I would have to get answers to the questions still troubling me. Just when I was supposed to 'let go' and 'move on' I felt I had to ask questions, the answers to which often went right over my head. The questions I asked were not dissimilar from those I asked about relatives. When my aunt was dying she was able to tell me how she felt. She told me she was tired of life and that she really wanted to die. Being able to approach one's death in this way is a consolation for everyone. Without making any judgements about how proper is the comparison, animals are unable to share accounts of their mental or physical experience of illness and dying. If I have grasped the fact of my cat's sentience and awareness and I have shared this in some way yet to be explained, then I want to understand what mental or physical experience my cat underwent. To try to understand this I asked different people, the local vet, the animal hospital vet, the manager at the RSPCA, the nurse. I asked them the same questions and this helped me get a comprehensive grasp of what happened to Harry. It also helped me test the veracity of the answers I was given and I needed to do this so that I could *finally live with them. At some stage I had all or most of my questions answered and by that stage I found I was already letting go of the past. There will always be doubts and these pull me in that backwards direction. But those doubts have become like all those day-to-day doubts that can be put aside without really understanding.*

In my opinion this is a perfect example, beautifully and painfully expressed, of a man coming to terms with a loss. Where he differs from many men (and women) is in his ability to communicate his feelings so well in writing. I also feel it shows a tremendous need to gain control of something he couldn't control. He couldn't tell his cat how he felt; therefore it was imperative that the gentleman found out, to the best of his ability, what Harry was experiencing just prior to his death. He felt he could only move on if he accepted that he had done everything to prevent unnecessary suffering (according to the experts) and provided the best possible emotional and physical support at the end. I wrote about grief and pet bereavement in *Cat Confidential* and I wish I had had the opportunity to discuss Harry then. This man truly loved his cat; his personality was such that he had to face the tough questions we all ask ourselves at such a time. Where others may have skirted round them or dwelled for a while without being able to be proactive, he tackled difficult subjects head on. This man saw the incredible nature of the cat as companion and friend and he wasn't afraid to express his feelings when he lost him. I can relate personally to his approach because I feel that I have tackled bereavement on several occasions in an equally 'aggressive' way. We all face this most difficult of times in the way that best suits our life experiences and our personalities. Whether it is entirely healthy to look for answers and be so hard on ourselves about our potential failings at the end is debatable. I hope that I was able in some small way to help this gentleman on his journey; I so want him to forgive himself for something that wasn't his fault.

Men are perfectly capable of loving cats too; I am absolutely convinced of that. It just happens in smaller numbers and, like most matters of the heart, they rarely speak of it. Most men, in my experience, are also more likely to view problems within the human/cat relationship with a much more black and white attitude than women. They will love the cat until it soils on the duvet or attacks a visitor. Their partner will become upset and the man will do what he does best: offer a solution. This solution usually is something like 'the cat's gone wrong so it has to go'. Whilst this looks great on paper it hardly represents a workable compromise. Many partnerships are at breaking point by the time I get involved for just this reason. They want their loved ones to stop hurting but the best answer they can find is to remove the problem, i.e. the cat. Behaviour therapy is usually perceived as complete mumbo jumbo ('You can't possibly train cats; they're not dogs') and I consider myself very fortunate if the husbands are even present when I arrive for the consultation. If they are, I know it's going to be OK because, with very few exceptions, they catch on quickly. They soon realize that the combination of a solution that means the cat can stay and Brownie points for showing willing is a complete win/win situation!

Just to add credence to my male cat lover argument, research conducted in 2004 by Dr June McNicholas for Cats Protection showed an even more positive picture of the modern cat/man relationship. In the UK today apparently there are 1.28 million male cat owners. I really do feel this is a product of the pressures on men to be something else – they had become 'indoctrinated' by society to be 'in touch with their feminine side' and more sensitive – but maybe this is a simplistic reasoning behind a very modern phenomenon. Dr McNicholas's research showed that single men are almost as likely as single women to consider choosing their cat over a partner or friendship. Since most of the men I come into contact with in my work are part of the man/woman/cat triangle it is difficult to comment on these statistics. I would, however, say that the single men I have met really are capable of loving their cat as intensely as any woman is. The research also showed that women are more attracted to men who like animals and male cat lovers are perceived to be nicer and more caring than the rest, so I would suggest that acquiring a cat is a good strategic move for any single man!

It is what it is

I love the expression 'it is what it is'. It perfectly describes how we should all ultimately feel about the relationships we have with our cats. Trying to understand the finer psychological elements of an inter-species partnership like ours is probably doomed to failure (but fascinating all the same). The best thing we can all do is accept the unique nature of every relationship between human and cat. I also believe that it is essential to the success of the partnership that we ensure we take time out to love our cats *their* way. Then everyone's happy.

CHAPTER 10

The Relationship Survey

I ALWAYS INTENDED THIS BOOK TO OFFER A VOICE TO THE CAT-owning public. This isn't just about how *I* feel; *Cat Counsellor* should reflect the human/cat relationship from a much broader perspective. It is perfectly valid for me to form my own opinions through my work and my own experiences (this is a very subjective topic) but I needed to open up a forum for the debate. The easiest way to achieve this was to conduct a survey to find out how cat lovers really feel about their pets. I compiled a questionnaire and placed it on my website (www.vickyhalls.net) and in the back of my last book, *Cat Detective*, hoping that owners would allow me a little insight into their relationships with their cats. The bulk of the questionnaire included statements against which the owners had to tick either AGREE, DISAGREE or NOT SURE to show their response. Many of the questions I asked were about emotions and feelings and sometimes it is difficult to be objective about ourselves and how we behave. I was not surprised to find a number of owners who completed the survey seeming to show incredible ambivalence as they agreed with two statements about their relationship with the cat that were the exact opposite of each other. Some owners ticked the NOT SURE box on just about everything. I actually think this is an extremely honest approach since a great deal of our relationship is taken for granted and rarely analysed. I personally found that the more I thought about a question, the more likely the answer was to change. The 'knee jerk' response to the statement was often not the true one. There are always going to be limitations to this sort of survey but I was still delighted with the response and I have included here the initial results from the first 150 completed questionnaires to help us all better understand this relationship phenomenon.

About you:

Age: 18–30 31%, 31–40 27%, 41–50 21%, 51–60 13%, 61+ = 8%

Sex: male 4%, female 96%

Marital status: married/cohabiting 58%, single (never married) 34%, divorced/separated 7%, widowed 1%

No. of children living at home: 0 88%, 1 7%, 2 5%, 3+ 0%

Working: full-time 72%, part-time 15%, retired 5%, not working 5%, unable to work 3%

No. of cats in household: 1 41%, 2 37%, 3 14%, 4 5%, 5 0%,
   6 0%, 7+ 3%
Any other pets?: Yes 24%, No 76%

The first set of questions was to establish the demographics of the survey. I wasn't surprised to see that the majority of those completing the questionnaire were women. I target women specifically, sometimes subconsciously, in my writing, lecturing and during my consultations and I feel these results have validated that approach. I will not dismiss the male as an unworthy cat lover, however, and I hope I have allowed them to have their say throughout this book.

It would be a perfect stereotype to show the typical cat lover as a single female who has never married but this clearly isn't the case. I have actually known this for some years, since the majority of my clients are married or living with a partner. Certainly a third of those surveyed were single but a greater percentage of owners were not living alone. The majority of the owners had no children living at home; is this significant? I have certainly worked with many women whose cats have been their 'children' until the real thing comes along; more of the 'child substitute' debate later.

Nearly three-quarters of those surveyed were working full-time, adding weight to the theory that people own cats because they work and therefore cannot have a high-maintenance dog. I am not convinced because I still subscribe to the view that there are defined cat lovers and dog lovers and a bunch of people who fall between the two extremes. A quarter of the cat owners had other species of pet too and I would probably describe them as part of that 'bunch'. However, it has to be said that I have other pets (a horse and a donkey) but I would consider myself to be a dyed-in-the-wool cat person!

I was gratified to see that 41 per cent of the owners had one cat. My views on multi-cat living are not a secret and I think you are fortunate if all the variables work in your favour and your cats get along. However, having just one cat does make it more likely that an intense bond can develop if the relationship is a true one-to-one sort of thing. I often think that my dear Puddy (my favourite cat, who passed away in 2002) and I would have been even closer if the other cats hadn't been around. (For those who haven't read *Cat Confidential*, I admit I was at one time the proud owner of seven cats. As a multi-cat household it worked fairly well because I benefited from a large home surrounded by fields and marshland and very little else. All individuals had plenty of opportunities to respect each other's personal space and things were largely peaceful. However, as I have said, variables such as environment and cat population density often conspire against the multi-cat household.)

About your cat:

Age of cat: < 2 yrs 28%, 3–5 yrs 27%, 6–8 yrs 29%,
    9–11 yrs 7%, 12+ yrs 9%
Sex: M(n) 55%, F(s) 41%, M(e) 0%, F(e) 4%
Pedigree/breed: domestic 74%, pedigree 26%

There was a nice cross-section of ages for the cats included in the survey. The ratio of 3:1 for moggies to pedigree does not reflect the total cat population but in this case it's probably appropriate. Pedigree owners have spent a great deal more money on the acquisition of their cats in the first place (that isn't necessarily a sign of the ultimate cat lover) and they tend to be enthusiastic and proactive owners since they have a certain expectation of their pet to behave as befits the breed. It was good to have a great mix: everything from Sphynx to Ragdoll and all variations in between.

Indoor/outdoor:

My cat has unlimited access outdoors: 31%
My cat has access outdoors but I shut him/her in at night: 36%
My cat has restricted access outside under supervision: 12%
My cat is taken out for a walk on a harness and lead: 5%
My cat is kept indoors but has an outdoor pen: 6%
My cat has access outdoors but doesn't go out: 2%
My cat is kept exclusively indoors: 8%

Forty-eight per cent of those surveyed restricted their cats' access outside and 19 per cent kept them exclusively indoors, took them for walks on a lead or contained them within an outdoor pen. Interestingly only 2 per cent had access outside but chose not to go out. The density of the cat population in certain urban areas is increasing daily and I am amazed that the less emotionally robust cats are not becoming agoraphobic in huge numbers.

What kind of relationship do you have with your cat?

My cat is a pet: 18%
My cat is a family member: 64%
My cat is like a child: 25%

My cat is a companion: 28%
I find it hard to explain my relationship with my cat: 1%

This was the first section that asked the owners to explore their feelings about their cats. Many of us will cohabit for years with various felines and never stop to question the type of kinship that has developed. Many owners specified more than one type of relationship, for example a child *and* a family member. This is perfectly valid and I admit that I would probably have ticked several of these boxes. Ironically, I would have ticked the box that said *I find it hard to explain my relationship with my cat* since, as such a deep thinker on the subject, I feel there are unique qualities within the cat/woman relationship that defy analysis and pigeon-holing. Only 1 per cent of those surveyed agreed with me!

The survey did confirm, however, the modern thinking that cats are gradually upgrading their status from pet to family member. This implies that the cat's perceived wishes are considered when making decisions, including those about holidays and moving house. I know of many owners who don't go away because the cat would be lonely, don't sit on the sofa because the cat's comfortable, get up in the middle of the night because the cat's bored and generally put themselves way down the list of priorities. That's some family member!

Over a quarter referred to their cat as a companion (but not a pet). If we consider our cats to be companions, without the proviso of also being pets, this surely implies equality by definition and describes a relationship with a degree of exclusivity? This is probably the modern definition of the human/cat relationship. By bestowing on them the title of 'pet' we are somehow denigrating their actual status as something much more than that. It is interesting to look at the dictionary definitions for both pet and companion: **Pet:** *1. a tame animal kept in a household for companionship, amusement, etc.* **Companion:** *1. a person who is an associate of another or others; comrade. 2. (esp. formerly) an employee, usually a woman, who provides company for an employer, esp. an elderly woman. 3. one of a pair; match.*

I often get castigated for using the terms 'own' and 'pet'; surely I should use more favourable phrases such as 'custodian', 'servant' or 'cohabiter'? I don't actually believe that stating 'I own a pet' is remotely derogatory. If you look at the dictionary definition above for 'pet' it is quite clear that that is *exactly* why most of us keep them (given that the et cetera will refer to all the other complex reasons why, known only to ourselves). Just because they are referred to as pets doesn't mean we do not care for them as well as anyone calling them something more serious on the scale of meaningful relationships. I'm probably labouring a point that is nothing more than confused or irrelevant terminology but defining the relationship has got to go some way towards understanding it and therefore ensuring it works for both parties.

A quarter of those surveyed referred to their cat exclusively as a 'child'. I am not convinced that all those who see their relationship in this way are merely biding time until they have a real baby with slightly less fur. Many women I have spoken to personally have chosen not to have children but still refer to their cats in a maternal way. I think this has a great deal to do with our innate programming as nurturers. Whether we make the decision to pursue careers instead of families or remain childless for another reason we still need to perform the role of mother for which we were designed. Just as cats will hunt shoelaces or rolled-up pieces of newspaper when they cannot be predacious, maybe we, as female humans, need to simulate natural maternal behaviour? It is also infinitely easier to practise parenthood on cats since the need for consistency and leading by example are mainly irrelevant and therefore you can perform all the enjoyable and simplistic elements of being a mother without the serious responsibility of helping to mould a brand-new person. Admittedly breeders do have more of a responsibility in that respect than most of us but it really isn't on quite such a grand scale.

Safety

I worry that my cat will come to harm when he/she is outside: AGREE 79%, DISAGREE 13%, NOT SURE 8%

I worry about the dangers of traffic: AGREE 82%, DISAGREE 13%, NOT SURE 5%

I worry that my cat may go missing: AGREE 76%, DISAGREE 15%, NOT SURE 9%

I worry about my cat fighting with others and getting injured: AGREE 67%, DISAGREE 25%, NOT SURE 8%

I worry that someone may steal him/her: AGREE 46%, disagree 43%, NOT SURE 11%

I like to know where he/she is at any given time: AGREE 61%, DISAGREE 29%, NOT SURE 10%

One thing that parenthood prepares us beautifully for is worrying. However, this emotion isn't the exclusive domain of those who think of their cats as children. Nearly 80 per cent of those surveyed worry about their cat coming to harm when outside the safety of the home. Many of these have actually confronted this fear and decided to restrict their pets' access outdoors. Roughly the same percentage were concerned about the dangers of traffic and their cats going missing but less than half believed that getting stolen was an issue for concern. Fighting or injuries worried two-thirds of the owners and almost the same number were only happy when they knew exactly where their pet was at any given time. This is something that is apparent in almost every case I have seen over the years. The owner's love for the cat is so intense that the fear of loss is equally great. It is why my age-old plea 'if you love them enough, then let them go' will always fall on deaf ears. Love is very difficult to view from an altruistic standpoint; I am not entirely sure if true altruism is even possible. We perceive our love in such a way that it revolves around our own pleasure. We do something that we think gives our cats pleasure therefore we are happy. These things rarely give us pain because, coincidentally, we believe that their pleasure is our pleasure. It is possible to argue that the person who cooks fish at 3 a.m. because that's when the cat wants it can hardly be having fun. The interesting point here is that it is the owner who has decided that this has to be done otherwise the cat will suffer in some way. The reality is quite the opposite but if we decide for ourselves what constitutes pleasure and happiness for our cats it can, due to the obvious 'lost in translation' element to the communication, only be judged by our own interpretation and beliefs. I think what I am trying to ask in a very roundabout way is 'If we restrict our pets access to the great outdoors because *we* are worried, are we considering *their* feelings and needs?' I don't dispute that they may well live longer, but will they be happy?

Interaction

I approach my cat for interaction more than he/she approaches me: AGREE 20%, DISAGREE 65%, NOT SURE 15%

My cat approaches me for interaction more than I approach him/her: AGREE 20%, DISAGREE 60%, NOT SURE 20%

My cat and I approach each other an equal number of times throughout the day: AGREE 65%, DISAGREE 24%, NOT SURE 11%

Sometimes my cat will ignore me or seem uninterested when I approach: AGREE 50%, DISAGREE 44%, NOT SURE 6%

I will respond to my cat at any time of the day or night: AGREE 60%, DISAGREE 35%, NOT SURE 5%

I always respond to my cat's approaches: AGREE 65%, DISAGREE 31%, NOT SURE 4%

I will check to see where my cat is if I haven't seen him/her for a while: AGREE 93%, DISAGREE 5%, NOT SURE 2%

I will occasionally wake my cat up to stroke him/her: AGREE 46%, DISAGREE 48%, NOT SURE 6%

I will seek my cat out if he/she is hiding: AGREE 52%, DISAGREE 39%, NOT SURE 9%

My cat will seek me out if I go into another room: AGREE 71%, DISAGREE 22%, NOT SURE 7%

My cat is by my side most of the time I am home: AGREE 41%, DISAGREE 53%, NOT SURE 6%

I can't sit down without my cat jumping on my lap: AGREE 26%, DISAGREE 65%, NOT SURE 9%

I talk to my cat occasionally at feeding times: AGREE 61%, DISAGREE 32%, NOT SURE 7%

I talk to my cat all the time: AGREE 80%, DISAGREE 15%, NOT SURE 5%

I hardly ever talk to my cat: AGREE 1%, DISAGREE 91%, NOT SURE 8%

My cat is very vocal and 'talks' back: AGREE 66%, DISAGREE 25%, NOT SURE 9%

In this particular section I was trying to ascertain how the owner and cat interacted on a day-to-day basis. Were the owners chasing harassed cats round the house or were the cats really hanging on their every word and not leaving them alone? It appears that the general consensus of opinion showed that contact was initiated equally between cat and owner in at least two-thirds of the households.

I was particularly interested in the results of the next few questions because they went a small way towards reinforcing my theory about why cats *really* turn women on (see the previous chapter). Half the people surveyed agreed that their cats occasionally ignore them or seem uninterested when they approach. Sixty per cent responded to their cats' wishes any time of the day or night, 65 per cent always responded to their cats no matter what they were doing and practically everyone went wandering round the house looking for their cats if they hadn't seen them for a while! Nearly half of the owners even woke their cats up to give them a stroke and a similar number will drag them out from cupboards or under the bed if they are hiding. I honestly believe if a cat is hiding it is doing it for a reason and whilst ill health is a possible cause it is just as likely to be having a private moment that should be respected as such. These last few questions relate to a lot of extra owner-to-cat approaches. I wonder whether the true picture of who initiates contact really shows the equal fascination that the majority of the owners describe? Just a thought!

The next three questions give a better insight into the cat's behaviour round its owner. Nearly three-quarters of the owners agreed that their cats would actually seek them out if they went into another room. Forty-one per cent were constantly by their owner's side and over a quarter couldn't wait for their owner to sit down to plonk themselves on their laps.

The vast majority of the owners were clearly talking a great deal to their cats and a significant majority of cats (although not quite so many) talked back. I received one letter from a talkative owner who wrote: *Most people think I am totally nuts about Jasper, talking to him like a human being, but as the saying goes, 'The more people I meet the more I like my cat.' That couldn't be more true.* I hear this sentence so often from cat lovers; sad really, because I don't think the love of humans and cats should be mutually exclusive. Only 1 per cent of the owners rarely spoke to their cats; I find it extraordinary that anyone would remain mute in the presence of a cat. Whilst most of us believe that their ability to understand English is minimal, we as humans communicate verbally and it would be impossible to form a relationship with another creature without doing so (unless we physically cannot). I say some crazy things to my cat Mangus; I am completely aware that she doesn't understand but she does appreciate the emotion behind the words and she enjoys the attention. She, like most other cats, will 'talk' back because it reinforces the attention and guarantees more of the same. Cats are not daft; talking means attention and attention means food or something equally pleasant.

Bedtime

My cat sleeps with me on the bed: AGREE 58%, DISAGREE 34%, NOT SURE 8%

I shut my cat out of the bedroom at night: AGREE 18%, DISAGREE 75%, NOT SURE 7%

My cat is given the choice but chooses to sleep elsewhere at night: AGREE 32%, DISAGREE 55%, NOT SURE 13%

My partner doesn't like my cat sleeping with us: AGREE 14%, DISAGREE 70%, NOT SURE 16%

I don't want my cat sleeping with me: AGREE 11%, DISAGREE 75%, NOT SURE 14%

Part of the whole relationship thing takes place at night. Many cats love to sleep with their owners, but don't be fooled. Their motivation is often warmth, security and familiarity of odour representing safety. Occasionally your company is useful at night when they get bored and start poking your nostril with their claws to see what happens. Just have a look at how much bed you are actually left with to see if there is any consideration for *your* needs at night-time!

Over half of the owners slept with their cat at night. A third of the owners gave their cat the choice but they chose to sleep elsewhere. Now I think I've seen a flaw in these statistics. If 18 per cent of owners shut their cats out of the bedroom at night and a total of 25 per cent either don't want their cat sleeping with them or have partners that think that way, simple maths tells me that there are some cats somewhere who are really getting their own way.

Personality

My cat is loving and attentive: AGREE 90%, DISAGREE 5%, NOT SURE 5%

My cat is sociable with everyone: AGREE 36%, DISAGREE 57%, NOT SURE 7%

I am the only person my cat wants to be with: AGREE 15%, DISAGREE 82%, NOT SURE 3%

My cat is very confident: AGREE 42%, DISAGREE 37%, NOT SURE 21%

My cat is self-reliant: AGREE 55%, DISAGREE 28%, NOT SURE 17%

My cat is needy: AGREE 30%, DISAGREE 50%, NOT SURE 20%

My cat can be aloof: AGREE 38%, DISAGREE 51%, NOT SURE 11%

My cat is very timid: AGREE 23%, DISAGREE 71%, NOT SURE 6%

This was always going to be a difficult section to complete because assessment of character and personality is incredibly subjective. I left the owners with a dilemma: for example, their cats may love one moment and be aloof the next. These traits are not mutually exclusive and I would hope that, from the results, most of the owners could see that these elements of their cats' personality are rarely exhibited all the time.

Ninety per cent of owners agreed that their cats were loving and attentive. A third of the cats were sociable with everyone but 15 per cent only wanted one specific person, their owner. One owner wrote: *Kim has never played and does not like people very much, but with me he is completely happy and I think I am blessed with a companion who is as near human as any animal could be.* She obviously feels immensely flattered that she has been singled out as the one person worthy of attention and this must feel good. It is also interesting to note that she refers to her companion as nearly human; this seems like the perfect compromise. A pseudo-human with all the positive traits, none of the negative and loads of soft fur! I've seen many cats who only want one person; this is often the result of poor early socialization or a complete lack of it. Some hand-reared cats bond exclusively with their carers and timid cats never get used to strangers if their owners have infrequent visitors.

Forty-two per cent of owners said their cats were confident and over half those surveyed agreed that their cats were self-reliant. This is encouraging since these are probably the two best qualities to prepare a cat for a life as a domestic pet. Thirty per cent agreed that their cats were needy. In our quest for the ultimately dog-like cat we try to breed selectively for sociability. As I have said before, this sometimes creates a dependent personality rather than a sociable one. It looks the same (lots of attention, etc.) but nearly a third of the owners appeared to see it for what it really is. Neediness is not a positive trait in cats; it puts enormous strain on the owner and, if left unchecked, can be the cause of much anxiety for the cat (see Chapter 8 for further details).

Twenty-three per cent of the cats were described as timid. Whilst a healthy suspicion of all novel things is a good survival strategy it is not in the animal's best interests to spook at every sudden noise or movement. These are tough cats to live with (see Chapter 6) and often, dare I say it, fairly unrewarding pets. The amount of love and attention given by the owners is never in proportion to the stuff they get in return. If you are looking for the whole 'unconditional love' thing these are probably not the cats for you.

Relationship

My cat knows what I am thinking: AGREE 25%, DISAGREE 49%, NOT SURE 26%

My cat understands when I am ill: AGREE 61%, DISAGREE 25%, NOT SURE 14%

My cat understands when I am depressed: AGREE 58%, DISAGREE 25%, NOT SURE 17%

My cat responds adversely when I am stressed: AGREE 35%, DISAGREE 45%, NOT SURE 20%

My cat would miss me terribly if I went away: AGREE 49%, DISAGREE 25%, NOT SURE 26%

My cat prefers my company to anyone else's: AGREE 46%, DISAGREE 40%, NOT SURE 14%

My cat understands what I am saying: AGREE 41%, DISAGREE 27%, NOT SURE 32%

My cat has a sense of humour: AGREE 48%, DISAGREE 30%, NOT SURE 22%

My cat would struggle to cope without me: AGREE 18%, DISAGREE 63%, NOT SURE 19%

I would struggle to cope without my cat: AGREE 63%, DISAGREE 24%, NOT SURE 13%

I wouldn't rehome my cat even if I knew he/she would be happier somewhere else: AGREE 15%, DISAGREE 49%, NOT SURE 36%

Nobody would care for my cat like I do: AGREE 43%, DISAGREE 35%, NOT SURE 22%

At this point in the survey I felt that the owners were sufficiently absorbed to be prepared to look at the deeper elements of their relationship. Twenty-five per cent of the owners truly believed that their cats knew what they were thinking. Interestingly, 26 per cent more were not sure whether they did or didn't. This is a tricky one since it is quite obvious that cats don't read minds. However, they are capable of the most incredibly accurate interpretation of the most subtle body language or changes in our tone of voice and this will often give them a very good impression of what we are thinking. If the question was asked on that basis – *Is your cat so tuned into your behaviour that it appears he can read your mind?* I would probably have ticked AGREE. Later in this section the owners were asked if they thought their cats understood what they were saying. This is another example of their accurate interpretation of non-verbal cues rather than their ability to speak English.

Forty-one per cent agreed that they did understand and a hefty third of the total number sat on the fence again, prepared to keep an open mind about the whole thing because sometimes it certainly seemed that they did.

Many people I have spoken to refer to instances when their cats have shown tremendous consideration for their feelings. One owner sent me a letter about the importance of her cat to the family when nobody else could help. She wrote: *His undemanding, uncritical affection has been a lifeline for depressed members of the family, for whom human communication has been impossible.* Over half of those surveyed agreed that their cats understood when they were ill or depressed and gave them comfort. One lady wrote: *If Gem had been human she would have been a hospital matron. Whenever my father was ill she stayed with him, stroking his face with the back of her paw. Since Father's death, over which she grieved for about six months, she has watched over me.* It is hard to imagine how another human could get this so right at such a difficult time.

Over a third of the owners felt that their stress impacted on their cats. I have seen many cases in my career where the owners' stresses have made life even tougher for their cats, who are already dealing with something else much more on a cat level. If the cat has a strong bond with the owner, then any stress that is perceived will look as if the owner is being affected by the same perception of threat that the cat is feeling. They don't see it being caused by a problem at the office; it's always going to be about them.

Nearly half of the owners agreed that their cats would miss them terribly if they went away. This is another factor that influences the owners' perception of their relationship with their cats. Loving someone means missing them if they are not around, therefore the cats must miss them because they love them. Many cats do miss the presence of their owners since it represents a significant change in the social dynamics of the household if the neighbour pops in to feed them and the familiar routines are absent. It can also mean a visit to the local cattery, which represents a twofold change, both social and environmental. I genuinely do believe, having said all that, that cats can form strong bonds and miss their owners terribly. I always feel more comfortable, however, if they stop short of actually fretting and becoming seriously anxious.

Just for fun I asked if the owners felt their cats had a sense of humour. Without exception I have found cat people to possess a sharp wit and many of the things cats do can be extraordinarily funny. Nearly half said they agreed that their cats had a sense of humour and another 22 per cent weren't sure. I just think they appeal to the incredible sense of humour that we cat lovers seem to have.

I then went back to the concept of loving and losing and suggested that their cats would struggle to cope without them. Sixty-three per cent realistically disagreed with this statement, understanding that they really weren't the centre of their cats' universe. This is exactly how it should be since if our cats want us rather than need us it makes it so much easier for them to function normally. Sadly and rather disturbingly exactly the same percentage of owners felt differently when asked if they would struggle to cope without their cats. Sixty-three per cent agreed they would. This is an example of the sort of letter I receive from people finding it difficult to come to terms with the death of their cat: *These companions, like no others, give us unquestioning love, devotion and the privilege of sharing their lives, so long as they are treated with the respect due to them. The loss of these precious friends leaves a hole in one's heart that can never be replaced. Indeed it is as if a part of us passes away with them. And yet, if we really search, our dear friends can still be seen, in the home and garden. They are young again, free, well and happy to be with us – for ever, if we want. First we must look and listen. They will always be there, patiently waiting for us. It is all we can ask and hope for.* This distresses me deeply because you can almost feel the writer desperately trying to create scenarios in her mind that make the absence of her pet more bearable. It is by far the easiest thing to believe they are still there, and a perfectly normal stage of the grieving process.

The next question goes back to the age-old challenge: do you love your cat enough to let him go? Fifteen per cent of the owners agreed that they wouldn't rehome their cat even if they knew he would be happier elsewhere. Nearly half, however, disagreed, implying they would. The rest honestly admitted that they weren't sure how they would react, given that situation. I would love to think that we are all capable of such selfless love that we would rehome our cat if it was unhappy. The reality, however, is very different. I think the key to this is the word 'know'. I honestly believe that if we could know beyond doubt that our cats would benefit from rehoming we would do it, albeit reluctantly. On the rare occasion that I have to recommend this to a client, the 'know' part is purely my advice. I hope that nobody finds themselves in this situation but it takes a very strong person indeed to sacrifice their own needs for those of the cat. Ironically, owners who give up their cats are often judged as poor owners or so unattached to their pets that they are making a decision based solely on convenience. In my experience this is almost always not the case and the individuals who have been forced to make this decision are punished twofold, by losing a loved pet and being castigated for it by all and sundry.

Forty-three per cent of the owners felt that nobody else would care for their cats as well as they did. A third of the owners disagreed and 22 per cent were not sure. Going too far down the line of believing that we have the exclusive rights to perfect cat care is dangerous. Many of those people who are referred to as 'collectors' suffer from this delusion. The RSPCA, the police and the council all become involved in removing large numbers of animals from tiny dwellings, many suffering from appalling neglect. These owners have created their own private 'rescue' centre and misguidedly believe that they are the only people who can save and protect their charges. The truth is quite the opposite and these poor souls are suffering from a recognized mental illness. I am not saying for one moment that those owners taking part in the survey who agreed with the statement *Nobody would care for my cat like I do* are certifiable! I just believe that there are numerous ways to express love for your pet and it is possible to get it right in more than one situation; it is also possible to take the 'nobody would care for my cat like I do' thought to an unhealthy extreme.

Love and support

My cat has given me comfort at a particularly difficult time in my life: AGREE 71%, DISAGREE 21%, NOT SURE 8%

My cat has supported me through bereavement: AGREE 34%, DISAGREE 53%, NOT SURE 13%

My cat has supported me through a relationship breakdown: AGREE 19%, DISAGREE 70%, NOT SURE 11%

My cat has supported me through illness: AGREE 45%, DISAGREE 48%, NOT SURE 7%

My cat feels unconditional love for me: AGREE 49%, DISAGREE 25%, NOT SURE 26%

My cat feels cupboard love for me: AGREE 22%, DISAGREE 40%, NOT SURE 38%

My cat's love is conditional on the way I treat him/her: AGREE 32%, DISAGREE 54%, NOT SURE 14%

My cat doesn't love me: AGREE 3%, DISAGREE 86%, NOT SURE 11%

My cat's love is very different from the expression of human love: AGREE 84%, DISAGREE 7%, NOT SURE 9%

My cat seems to love me sometimes but not others: AGREE 26%, DISAGREE 58%, NOT SURE 16%

If I don't do what my cat wants he/she won't love me any more: AGREE 1%, DISAGREE 93%, NOT SURE 6%

My cat will still love me even if I rejected him/her occasionally: AGREE 88%, DISAGREE 5%, NOT SURE 7%

This set of questions referred to the most complex of emotions: love. I asked first whether their cats had helped them through a difficult time in their lives. Seventy-one per cent agreed that their cats had been a great comfort to them. Thirty-four per cent had been supported through bereavement, 20 per cent through a relationship breakdown and 45 per cent through illness. This is an extract from a typical letter showing how important a cat's support is at a traumatic time: *My cat has been such a friend and stayed close to me ten years ago when my husband left us. He shadowed me for weeks, months, only leaving me when I had visitors to keep me company. He is a real gentleman.*

I then made the classic statement *My cat feels unconditional love for me* and asked for the owners' reactions. Nearly half agreed that their cats did indeed show unconditional love but the rest disagreed with the statement or were unsure about its validity. Many people refer to the love of a pet as unconditional but I think you will have seen by now that I think it is far more complicated than that. I personally wouldn't feel comfortable in a relationship where the other party showed 'unconditional love'. This suggests in my mind that the love is somehow undervalued because my behaviour within the relationship is irrelevant. I understand the appeal of being loved 'warts an' all' but surely we still have to make *some* effort?

I then made the rather more cynical statement that cats show 'cupboard' love; we are merely large tin openers, chicken cookers and packet rippers. Only 22 per cent agreed with me and I'm rather glad about that because this may be a strong motivation for cats but it certainly isn't the whole story. The next statement, *My cat's love is conditional on the way I treat him*, seemed to me to be a far healthier perception of our role in the relationship. Only a third agreed and 54 per cent disagreed. It is not surprising to see that this is a similar percentage to those who believed in cats' unconditional love so I obviously wasn't making any headway with them!

When I suggested that a cat's love is very different from the expression of human love a resounding 84 per cent agreed. I think this is an incredibly important point since it could show the general disillusionment that many people feel about human relationships. As I have said before, the human/cat equivalent is capable of mimicking many of the best bits without the constant disappointments that loving another human seems to create. Cats are very compliant in this respect; it is clear from all the anecdotal evidence that cats are delighted to perform this role and be whatever we want them to be in our heads. As long as there is a friendly face, a warm bed and a good meal they are fairly laid back about the complexities of the emotional undertones.

Once again working on the theme of partial reinforcement, I suggested that some cats seemed to love their owners sometimes and not others. Over a quarter of the owners agreed with me but most were convinced the love was consistent despite their responses to similar statements earlier in the questionnaire.

Only 1 per cent agreed that their cats wouldn't love them any more if they didn't do what they wanted. A huge 93 per cent disagreed – that love really *is* unconditional! Joking apart, it is also quite healthy because it is entirely right that we shouldn't always do what our cats want. Eighty-eight per cent thought their cats would still love them if they rejected them occasionally and this also is absolutely the right attitude. Attention-seeking problems are rarely present in households where the owners understand this principle.

Behaviour problems

My cat has shown aggression towards another cat in the household: AGREE 34%, DISAGREE 56%, NOT SURE 10%

My cat has shown aggression towards me or another person: AGREE 28%, DISAGREE 68%, NOT SURE 4%

My cat has soiled in the house: AGREE 23%, DISAGREE 77%, NOT SURE 0%

My cat has sprayed urine in the house: AGREE 13%, DISAGREE 86%, NOT SURE 1%

My cat has been treated for a behaviour problem: AGREE 5%, DISAGREE 93%, NOT SURE 2%

Since I am a cat behaviour counsellor I had to take this opportunity to check that all was well at home from a behavioural perspective. The majority of the owners disagreed with statements concerning aggression and soiling but regrettably (but not surprisingly) a third of the cats had been aggressive to others in the household, nearly a third had been aggressive towards humans, 23 per cent had soiled indoors and 13 per cent had sprayed urine. In yet another example of our incredible power to tolerate and forgive, only 5 per cent of those surveyed, despite the significant number of problems, had sought professional help.

I shall leave the last word in this chapter to you. I asked at the end of the questionnaire how the person would summarize their feelings for their cat in fifty words or less. Here are a few examples of your replies.

Rosie is the joy of my life. Having no children I feel she is my child. Rosie is a cat amongst cats – I cannot think of a single thing she does that makes me angry. Life without her will be very difficult for me. I have had other Siamese, great cats, but Rosie is and always will be very, very special.

I feel unconditional love for her – however I don't like her outside too long and feel I am a 'mean Mum' BUT when I have to go out for 1–2 hours she appears to dislike it and will play me up, refusing to come in or acknowledge my calling her! So, I don't go out a great deal any more, as her reaction distresses me!

She is like a little child. Sometimes I can love and hate her at the same time. She is constantly on my mind when I am away. I sometimes feel frustrated for not understanding what she wants. I love this little menace to bits.

I love him. He makes me laugh. He cheers me up. He has helped me through a difficult time and he is like a mobile comforter. But I don't smother him so I think we have the balance about right. Best friend, clown, comforter, toe-warmer but still a cat!

And my own personal favourite . . .

He's like my husband: lazy, eats constantly and getting more rotund by the years. I would not change a thing.

Epilogue

CAT COUNSELLOR HAS BEEN RATHER AN EMOTIONAL JOURNEY for me. Coincidentally, I have had the opportunity to personally evaluate a number of cat relationships in my own life. During the writing of this book I have lost another of my beloved cats in Cornwall (Bakewell) and started my very first one-to-one relationship with a cat (Mangus). I have embarked on a 'textbook' eternal triangle with Mangus and an allergic ailurophobe man and marvelled at the challenge it represents. The impact these relationships have on all three parties is profound.

If I had to sum up the unique flexibility of the cat and what it means to me, it would be thus. Cats are chameleons. They change themselves to suit the situation, with the overall objective to remain safe and get the most out of the environment and everything in it, and that includes the owners. The enigmatic nature of their responses and behaviour allows the owners to make of the relationship what they will. Whatever the cat is 'saying' with its body language and vocalization can be interpreted to suit the owner's perception of the relationship. For example, a cat with poor coping strategies for life can easily form a dependency on an owner that is unhealthy and not in his best interests. The owner sees a really friendly cat and remarks, 'He loves me so much he won't leave me alone, bless him,' all the while thinking, 'I must be a very special person for my cat to love me so much.' It is just as easy to misinterpret sedentary behaviour in the chronically anxious cat – an individual so distressed and unsure that he rarely moves but whom his owner describes as 'laid-back and chilled'. How easy it is to be misled by the companion we feel we know so well.

In my quest to spread a better understanding of our relationships with these special creatures I make no apologies for the serious nature of some of my comments in the last couple of chapters. I realize I have always preached that human/cat relationships should be fun but I don't believe this should be at the expense of the knowledge of what we are taking on. We are making ourselves responsible for the well-being of another creature and, therefore, we have a duty to appreciate the relationship for what it truly is and behave accordingly. These relationships should not merely be a reflection of what we long for or need; they should always be mutually beneficial. If you honestly believe that you respect your cat's need to be feline then I am delighted. You are doing your very best for your cat, and if I have contributed in any way to that understanding, I am deeply gratified.

I spend the vast majority of my life thinking about cats and our relationships with them. All opinions expressed in *Cat Counsellor* are nothing more than my own thoughts and musings. There is no perfect way to love a cat and I would tie myself up in knots if I tried to define it. I hope that, if nothing else, this book has made you think and re-evaluate your own opinions, particularly if you have been experiencing problems.

There are always going to be those who marvel at the fact that I have devoted a whole book to the relationship aspect of cat ownership. There are many people who consider the whole concept of human/cat relationships to be frivolous and self-indulgent and I respect their right to have this opinion. Ironically, even some owners with a low level of attachment to their pets have cats that are perfectly content. This is one fact that keeps coming back to me when I advise clients with unhappy or unruly cats to merely 'ignore them'. Loving your cat your way doesn't necessarily bring it happiness. Cats tend to work with what they are given and if an owner considers them to be nothing more than an impulse buy and a bit of a nuisance, cats can still make it work for them and go about their business unhindered. Those cats that remain true to their nature can easily survive in an atmosphere devoid of the sort of love that many humans consider essential. The whole thing goes wrong, however, when it comes to veterinary care, as low-attached owners are rarely prepared to pay the huge bills that many serious conditions merit. So maybe being 'cared for' by them does have its disadvantages.

This leads me to a depressing aspect of the human/cat relationship where the debate becomes even more complicated. Veterinary medicine has progressed incredibly over the past few years and procedures such as complicated heart surgery and kidney transplants are now being carried out. This creates a dilemma in my mind: is it right to elect for this sort of treatment for our cats just because we can? Is it worse for a cat to be humanely put to sleep as a result of severe injury or disease, rather than be treated painfully and stressfully for many months? We might be prolonging life but we are changing the cat's perception of the trustworthiness of humans for ever. Some cats cope well with lengthy veterinary treatment but many don't.

This really is a tough one; I personally would do anything for my cats but I am adamant that it must be *for* my cats and not for me. I believe that when and if we are ever faced with this sort of decision we should throw out the largely human drive to avoid death at all costs. Cats have no concept of their mortality; they do not fear death or have religious beliefs about the sanctity of life. They understand fear, pain and suffering and face death with resignation. This is a depressing debate but a fascinating one none the less. Making these sorts of decisions is all part of the relationship. Should our own sensitivities be uppermost when we find it hard to let go?

I promise that is my very last sombre note! Cats are fun and fascinating and so are cat owners and I say a big 'thank you' to everyone who has taken the trouble to write to me about their amazing companions. Every letter is read carefully and thoroughly enjoyed and each one illustrates the enormous variety that exists in cat personalities and cat/human relation- ships. Some owners are struggling with nervous cats and some feel terribly rejected when their cats resort to violence to get their own way. Most feel the failure is their own if something goes wrong and I doubt whether I will ever convince people that it is rarely that straightforward.

If you have tried loving your cat your way and feel you are failing maybe it would be worth taking a few moments to reflect on the true nature of your relationship with your cat. If in doubt, get to grips with what your cat actually wants and needs and try to show your love the feline way instead. Do let me know what happens!

Index

territory 58–9, 67–77
   defending of 63–7, 79, 148
   invasion through cat flap 65–6,
     67–73, 74–5, 179–80, 182
timid cats *see* nervous cats
Tom and Jerry 18
Top Cat 18
'treat them mean, keep them keen'
   philosophy 216–17
Trygul 10

'unconditional love' 245–6
urination 52–3, 56, 66, 70, 105, 180

veterinary medicine 252–3
Virgin Mary 10

Walker, Robin 24, 140, 202
wandering cats 61–3
Weir, Harrison 16–17
witches 14, 15, 16
women
   relationship with cats 10,
     11–12, 15, 213–16, 218,
     235

Zulu 44